ALL MY FRIENDS ARE INVISIBLE

ALL MY FRIENDS ARE INVISIBLE

When the world doesn't understand you, it's time to create your own

JONATHAN JOLY A MEMOIR

QUERCUS

First published in Great Britain in 2022 by

QUERCUS

Quercus Editions Ltd
Carmelite House
50 Victoria Embankment
London EC4Y 0DZ

An Hachette UK company

A CIP catalogue record for this book is available
from the British Library

HB ISBN 978 1 52942 057 9
TPB ISBN 978 1 52942 058 6
Ebook ISBN 978 1 52942 059 3

10 9 8 7 6 5 4 3 2 1

Typeset by CC Book Production
Printed and bound in Great Britain by Clays Ltd, Elcograf S.p.A

MIX
Paper from
responsible sources
FSC® C104740
www.fsc.org

Papers used by Quercus are from well-managed forests and other responsible sources.

This book is dedicated to all the invisible friends
who have saved kids just like me.

CONTENTS

Opening the Box

2016 (age thirty-six)

I've spent a lot of time trying to figure out where to start this story. I know that the beginning is probably the right place, but sometimes it takes a lifetime to realise the meaning behind your past. So maybe the best place is not at the beginning of me, but at the awakening of me, the trigger which sent me on the adventure back to Domdie, back to Giselle, and which ultimately led to me writing this book, for you.

It was 2016 and my wife Anna, our children Emilia (then four) and Eduardo (then three) and I were at Costa Coffee in Gatwick Airport. We were waiting to catch a plane to Ireland for my thirty-sixth birthday. At this point in my life, I had reached amazing career heights, I had a beautiful wife who was also my best friend, and two gorgeous children. I thought I was living the dream.

It was just like any other of the thousand times we had been in an airport together. We checked in, dropped the bags, managed the kids though security and then speed-walked through duty-free so that Anna wouldn't get distracted by all the things she didn't need. I had a system where I would give Anna an earlier time for a flight so that we would always get to the airport well ahead of departure. Oddly, no matter how many times I did this, she never caught on until we arrived at the airport, and then she'd get annoyed with me.

So, with time to kill we headed off to grab some breakfast. I ordered a green juice and a sausage roll, Anna got the porridge, and we ordered bananas and pastries for the kids. I sat with them as Anna waited to collect her porridge. Eduardo was trying to eat a croissant while Emilia was chatting away to me, when something strange happened. Something I hadn't experienced in a long time: I could see Emilia talking to me, but each word that came out of her mouth was muffled and became harder to hear, until I couldn't hear her at all. I looked at my hands and they didn't feel like my hands anymore. They started shaking, I was suddenly sinking into my chair, and a voice that I know I recognised, but hadn't heard in ages, whispered in my ear: 'Come.'

Sweat began to run down my face, and pain started to weave its way throughout my body. All of a sudden, my legs began to move beyond my control. I'd never had a heart attack before, or a stroke, and I wondered, *Is this what it feels like? Is this what people experience before they die?*

I looked up at my two beautiful babies, who were staring back at me, and I thought, *Is this it? Is this all I get with them? How will their life shape without me, how can this be the end?*

Life had only just started to get interesting, and I was not ready to say goodbye.

I stood up just as Anna came back to the table with her breakfast. She was looking at me, confused as to why I was getting up, why I was starting to leave without taking a child with me, as that is the kind of thing you do as a parent when you have more than one child – if you need the toilet, you take a child, you need to go to the post office, you take a child, and so on. But I didn't want to bring one of my children with me to watch me die, and how would I even choose which one to experience that with?

I couldn't explain how I felt to Anna even though she was the one person in my life that I had always been able to open up to, to share my deepest, most hidden secrets with. I didn't know if I was embarrassed or ashamed. I was the strong leader of our family, I was the one who protected Anna and our children, I was the one who didn't show weakness, and yet that's how I felt right now. I heard the voice again, repeating the same word: 'Come', but this time with more intensity. The pressure was building.

I tried to find the words to give some kind of explanation to Anna, but all I managed was: 'I have to go.'

I grabbed my phone and bolted out the door of the café. I was suddenly in a sea of people, all rushing to get to their gates, catch their planes, get on with their lives. While for me it felt like it might be the end of mine. But where was I rushing to? And would these people help me?

I started walking very quickly. I saw signs for the men's toilet, and I followed them for ages. Have you ever noticed how in airports, the signs for the toilet can sometimes be so far away from the actual place that you might as well wait until you're on the plane? I finally found the entrance.

I pushed open the half-wood, half-plastic bathroom door. Thankfully the room was empty, so I went into the first cubicle and sat down, still sweating, still shaking, with no idea what was going on. I pulled out my phone, but who was I going to call? And what would I say? Why did I leave Anna and the kids?

I opened and closed apps at random in an effort to distract myself. I was in full-on panic mode and I couldn't figure out how to get my mind to settle. I could hear people come into the toilet, talking, laughing, washing their hands. I homed in on the sound of the water flowing from the tap and hitting the sink with a splashing sound. It got louder and the hairs on the back of my neck started to stand up. I looked at the walls of my wooden cubicle, sheltering me from the outside world, and slowly a strange but familiar feeling began to surround me again.

I was in an airport toilet, yet I could smell fresh air, and the noise of the water from the tap was now the sound of a river flowing. The airport hum was fading into the background and being replaced by the sounds of a world I once lived in, a place I'd called home many years ago, a place I had forgotten.

I was no longer in Gatwick Airport, I was back inside Domdie . . .

All the distractions of my adult life had anchored me into my reality and kept me from Domdie, the alternate world I had spent most of my childhood in, the place that saved my life, the place where I felt connected to something. I couldn't remember when or why I stopped coming to Domdie, but here I was again.

I was sitting on a fallen oak tree and I could feel the bark against my legs and the grass between my toes. A cool breeze caressed my face. It brought calmness with it, but there was a hint of sadness too. Something was missing. I could feel that my memory of this beautiful world I used to visit as a child, which had remained dormant all these years, had faded with time. Without me visiting, the life force and energy of this place had been left to wither. Where it once had been full of the joyful sound of my friends' voices, there was now only an eerie silence.

Domdie was empty.

I took a step forward and paused.

What if with each step I took, I was sucked into Domdie as used to happen many years before? What if I couldn't find my way back? I was not the little boy who had nothing to lose, I didn't have an enemy that I needed protection from. I had a wife, kids, a life that I liked . . . Why was I here again?

I reached down and put my hand on the soil. The ground felt dry, like a neglected garden that hadn't been watered in a lifetime. I dug my fingers deeper under the dirt and I could sense a faint pulse, like a beating heart. I turned my head so that my ear was close to the ground – I wanted to hear what I could feel. I noticed a glimmer of metal beside me, poking out of the ground. As I pulled the object up, I realised it was the seat from a swing, the very seat from the double swing I used to sit on for hours, sometimes with Giselle and sometimes my other friends. They would hold me the way I longed for my mam to do but never did. I have no memories of her holding my hand, pushing me on a swing or telling me she loved me, yet I have in my mind a childhood full of such memories from inside Domdie.

Holding the swing in my hand, a forgotten memory started to play out, as if someone were projecting a movie in the space that surrounded me, and then another began. The longer I held on to it, the more memories played. These were all the experiences and moments in my childhood I had spent so long trying to forget, buried deep inside my mind, inside my forgotten world, but being here now was awakening them.

In the distance, between the movie memories, I saw what I could only describe as a fog, but brighter, like the air from your breath on a cold day. Its light emerged like a new sun rising over the mountains on the first day of spring, and it was moving closer to me.

A shape began to emerge from out of the fog. I saw a hand reaching out and I raised my hand instinctively. I didn't know what would happen next, but I needed to reach out too. As our hands touched, a wave of static energy sparked and restarted a forgotten connection and thirty years of deeper, hidden, locked-away emotions came flooding over me.

Was this Giselle?

I pulled her hand to me, bringing her fully out of the light and closer to me. The ground around us began to come alive again as if our connection was the life force of this world. The closer we got the more colour and life began to spread around us. We sat together on the fallen oak tree and the only words I could say were, 'Sorry I left.'

Giselle looked back at me, her hair still as blonde as I remembered, and while she had aged just like I had, we were also still both children at the same time, still holding hands just like we used to when trying to escape from the Enemy. Nothing and everything had changed. She leaned in and whispered, 'I never left you.'

I asked her the question that was on my mind.

'Why am I here? I understand why I needed this place as a child, why I needed you, but why am I here again? I don't understand.'

Giselle, who had her head resting on my shoulder, looked up at me and said, 'It's time to open the box.'

Before I had time to ask her what that meant, my phone rang and I was back in the toilet, alone and cold. I looked at my phone and I could see it was Anna calling me, and with each burst of my ring tone, Domdie receded back into the invisible.

I answered the phone.

'Hi. Sorry, I'm coming back now. I'll explain when I get there.'

I hung up and looked around. *Was that a dream?*

Walking back to the café, I watched the crowds of people still rushing around, running to catch their flights as if nothing had happened, as if nothing had changed. But for me everything had changed. I was once again in touch with Domdie, with Giselle. But why? I didn't think I felt disconnected like I used to. Was I disconnected?

I had spent the last thirty years convincing myself that this world I'd discovered wasn't real, and that Giselle and the others – my invisible friends who visited me when I was a child – weren't real. But if that were true then none of this happening right now made any sense.

Despite the questions in my head, I felt much calmer now, more relaxed. I thought I had been gone hours, but it had only been twenty minutes or so. As I approached the table, Anna was cleaning Emilia's face, so I just slipped back into Dad mode, wiped Eduardo's chocolate-covered mouth and got them back into their buggy. We caught our flight to Ireland, spent a week in Cork and I turned thirty-six years old.

A few weeks after getting back home, we found out we were expecting our third child. Thanks to this distraction, and what with having two other little ones to manage as well as a busy work schedule, I gave no further thought to Domdie and to what had happened at Gatwick. I got on with my life and focused on Anna's pregnancy.

Before I met Anna, I had no desire to have children. I didn't want anyone else to experience the life I'd had, and I thought the best way to keep that from happening was not to have any children. But thankfully Anna persisted, and Emilia was born, followed shortly by Eduardo, and those two kids changed my whole world. They showed me that pain wasn't set in stone, that I had the power to break the cycle and together we could all learn from each other. It was me who had encouraged Anna to have a third child. I loved our family unit. The happy family I had always yearned for myself was now a reality for me, so I wanted to grow it.

Sadly, at twelve weeks we found out that our little baby hadn't made it. I went from having a heart filled with hope to being overcome with sadness. I got a tattoo to honour the baby's memory, and one evening Anna and I released paper lanterns into the night sky. It may have seemed like an over-reaction but for me I needed to do something. I needed to express how I felt about losing a child.

We went on to have two more babies, a girl named Alessia in March 2017, and then a boy named Andrea in August 2018.

Then, in the summer of 2019, when all the excitement of having a new baby was settling down and life was getting back to normal, I started having night sweats. This went on for weeks. I would wake up every night completely soaked. I bought an electric fan to put beside my bed, but it didn't help at all. Nothing helped. It got to the point where I was laying out another pair of pyjamas and some towels for when I would wake in the night. It was very disruptive, and the lack of sleep was starting to affect my work.

I booked an appointment with a doctor who submitted me for blood tests and a physical observation. Apparently, there was nothing wrong with me. In my final appointment with this doctor, he started asking probing questions.

'Tell me, Jonathan, was there anything in your past that might explain how you feel now? Have you ever had any mental health issues or stress as a child?'

At first, I said no, because I think I genuinely believed there hadn't been, but then I said:

'Well actually, yes, there was this one thing . . . I went to a school for children with emotional problems. Does that count?'

I left his office with a prescription for antidepressants. I was hopeful that this was the answer to the night sweats issue, but I was also confused. It was as if I had been watching a television show for years and somebody had just told me that I had started the show in the middle and I had missed out on the whole beginning. Did I have mental health problems? Was I depressed?

I sat in my car outside the local Morrisons holding the prescription in my hand and trying to make sense of this. I wanted to get better, I wanted to get some sleep, but I also needed to know how I had got to this point. As I stared at the paper, reading the words over and over again, my mind racing through my life's memories, looking for meaning, I started to feel the same pressure building inside me that I had felt three years earlier at Gatwick. It was happening again; my heart was racing, pounding; sweat was creeping from my hairline. But this time it was different, I knew what was happening and I wasn't afraid.

Rather than feeling the helpless cold sense of impending death, I was feeling the warmth of a rebirthing. This wasn't the end of me, this was the beginning of something else . . . so I closed my eyes, took a deep breath, and leaned back into my seat, and as I did, I felt the air around me change, every hair on my body stood up, my breathing became more regular, my heartbeat slowed down . . .

I opened my eyes and found myself looking straight up at the sky above me, the trees swaying in the wind and coming into my line of vision, in and out, like metronome rods, keeping time. I was back in Domdie, but it wasn't like last time. There was a feeling of energy and life; something was stirring here.

I sat up and took a deep breath, and as the air filled my body, I felt calm and excited to be there, even though I still didn't know why I was back. Without fear, I started to walk. I reached a wooded area densely packed with tall thin trees. As I passed through, I laid my hand on the tree trunks, but instead of feeling the texture of bark I got a pulse of energy flowing from my hand to my heart to my head. Just like last time, I was given a memory: I was five years old and hiding under my bed in the room I shared with my brother. Giselle was next to me, trying to cheer me up. She was always there for me, helping me to survive.

With each tree I passed and touched, I was given another memory. This time I was seven years old, and I was talking to my mam about wanting to leave this world; I was broken and I couldn't see a way to fix my shattered young life. I started to run, touching every tree I could to open more and more memories. I was crying, I was laughing, I was running, I was unlocking the past I had forgotten.

I kept running until I ran out of the wooded area and into a large open space. For as far as I could see into the distance there was nothing, except . . . was that the swing? I walked to it and, taking the rope in my hand, lowered myself onto the seat. I looked over at Giselle who was suddenly sitting on the seat next to me. She stepped up, readying herself to swing forward.

'Are you ready?' she asked

I stood up, copying her, readying myself to swing. 'Yes,' I said, 'I am.'

We both smiled at each other for a moment and then in perfect sync we jumped forward to let the swing's momentum lift us out of Domdie and back into my car, parked outside Morrisons. I was still holding the prescription in my hand, but my mind was no longer searching for meaning. The adrenalin rush had faded away. I looked over at Giselle who was sitting beside me.

I turned the ignition. 'Let's go home.'

And now I know this: for the past thirty years, I hadn't been lying to others about who I was – I'd been lying to myself. I had hidden my true self under so many layers of personalities that the real me was never able to surface, never able to be heard due to a fear my childhood had instilled in me.

You see, I was born a boy, but on the inside, I was a girl. I wanted to wear my sisters' dresses, I wanted to play with girls, I wanted to *be* a girl. And while I fancied girls, I never thought of myself as gay or bisexual or trans (not that I knew what these words meant when I was younger). And how I dealt with that, and how people dealt with that, was very difficult.

It was especially hard for my parents. I don't hold anything against them anymore for their actions during the years I lived with them. To me as a child, Mam and Dad were more than just people, they were my everything, despite the problems we had.

At the same time, parents are of course just people, and people are flawed, so the relationship between them and their children can sometimes be destructive. If you're lucky, when you're a kid you find a means to cope. For me, that meant escaping to Domdie. And it was there that I was able to learn to forgive and to heal. Without my invisible friends or Domdie, I don't think I would have made it this far.

Projecting a personality that others could relate to was something I was unable to do before I became a teenager, and it was also because of that, that I ended up in Domdie. I created a place deep inside me, where I could live out my true identity. And this is the knowledge that I now know: that Giselle came back into my life to help me make my peace with those years, and to help others.

Giselle wasn't just a friend I'd made up, she *was* me. She was my inner voice, she brought me comfort when life got too hard to endure. As you will discover, she entered my world when I was three years old, and throughout my childhood, she visited me whenever I was frightened, felt lost or found my reality too difficult. She was the person I could hide behind. And she was different to the other invisible friends, who you will also meet, because she was the only one I could truly be myself with. Sometimes I would let her take over completely, and I would be the one hiding on the inside.

Even though I am no longer disconnected from this world, the world you know, for the first time in my life I am connected to both worlds. The connection to Giselle and my other invisible friends is stronger now than at any other time in my life; I visit them in Domdie and they visit me here.

I know for most people this will all sound crazy, and maybe I am crazy, but if being crazy is what it takes to survive, then I will happily accept that burden.

Perhaps you also have an invisible connection to someone or something to guide you through your disconnected moments or give you a place to escape or hide from your enemies. If so, this book is for you, this story is your story, and I hope it helps you. If you've never needed a place to escape to, let me tell you what it's like, and show you how I am alive and happy today.

CHAPTER 1

My First Friend

1983 (age three)

I'm sitting on a small chair at a round school table at Presentation Convent in Terenure, Dublin. It's a trial day to meet the teacher, because I am about to join junior school. My brother Simon, who is only one year older than me, goes to this school already. My big sister Ruth is in her last year in the lower end of the school. In Ireland they call this 'Low Babies' and 'High Babies', and I am about to join Low Babies.

My table seems huge to me. It is designed to fit a number of children, but there's only me, and I'm very small for my age. It is covered with dried, multi-coloured paint that looks like it might have been there since before I was born. I'm wearing Simon's uniform, which was Ruth's before him: a white shirt, a red jumper and a pair of grey trousers. Although Ruth did get to wear a grey skirt, which I would have much rather worn instead of the trousers. At the top of my white shirt, I am wearing a little red bow tie, and I am under strict orders not to mess with it.

As I child I was always more interested in being on my own. I never knew how to blend with the crowd or fit into the herd. I doubt I was the only person who felt how I did, but I didn't know how to spot the signs of other introverted kids, or maybe they were just better at hiding it than me. Later on, as an older child and even as a young adult, I would make up stories and tell lies about myself, projecting a fantasy of the person I thought people wanted me to be. I would act how I considered a normal person to act, based on my observations. But on this day, at three years old, I don't really have the life experience to guide me. So, while all the other children are making friends and chatting away, I sit alone.

I watch my mam talk to all the other new mams. Mam always had plans and aspirations for her children. Her philosophy was the polar opposite of the Charles Bukowski concept of 'don't try in order to succeed'. My mam tried as hard as she could to elevate us, and one of her great plans was to pair us up with the 'right' friends from the 'right' families, thus helping us to establish ourselves in the community, and in life.

There was one small flaw in this because my family had a secret: we were imposters, living in a middle-class road in south County Dublin. My parents had bought into the area early, before the well-to-do moved in and changed everything. But we were, in fact, still a working-class family. I'm sure there might have been a few more imposters like us who'd managed to sneak into the school like my family had, but the majority of the families at the school were the types who ate pork chops and had crisps in their lunch boxes – proper posh.

My father worked as a cabler for a Dublin-based 'pipe' television company. But back in the eighties the only cabling that was needed was to give people access to the three television channels Ireland had to offer: RTÉ 1, RTÉ 2 and UTV. The internet hadn't been invented yet, so television was the primary broadcast media option, but most families at that time couldn't justify the cost. My dad's income was very limited, but he stayed in the same job for the next fifteen years, until he was made redundant in 2002.

My parents met in December 1969 when Mam was seventeen years old and working as a nurse in Temple Street children's hospital. My father's father was Professor of Histology there, and that Christmas my grandfather decided to bring his only son, John, to the hospital Christmas party. That's how I came to exist.

My parents bought their first house in 1972 and then married the following year. My mam gave up her nursing career after welcoming her first daughter, Ruth, in 1977. Ruth was followed by Simon in 1978, me in 1980 and then finally Leah in 1983.

Some people marry for love, some marry for money and then there are the small few who marry to escape; my mam was one of those. She grew up in a hostile family environment with a mother who, up until her death a few years ago, maintained she never loved my mam.

My mam wasn't particularly affectionate either, but despite all the people in my life who looked past me, who thought I was too much work to fix, too hard to understand, she never gave up on me. No, we didn't have the best day-to-day friendship, but she always said, 'I'm not your friend, I am your mother,' which only made sense to me when I became a parent myself. She herself was trapped as a child, and made a promise that she would never let her own children be trapped. So what may have looked like calculated social climbing was, in fact, her survival training.

Which is why she is standing here in the classroom, using her charm and focus to identify the right friends to pair me up with. She looks over at me from time to time, making sure I am not doing anything to distort the picture of me she is undoubtedly painting. I am very aware that this is my audition to be part of the herd that I myself cannot gain entry to, so I must not do anything to mess it up for her. Personally, I'm not too concerned about fitting in as there isn't much about this world and its social norms that interests me, but I know it is important to her.

I look around the classroom at the artwork lining the walls and the rows of books propped up on the floor. There is a window across from me and I can see out into the playground and the faded remnants of a chalked hopscotch outline. The rest is just empty tarmac, surrounded by a high wall to the front and a net on either side to separate the school from the main convent.

I can also see my own reflection in the window, but then I notice it appears someone is sitting beside me. It's a girl. I hadn't noticed her before – was she sitting here the whole time, or did she just come over?

She looks about the same age as me, she has blonde hair down to her shoulders and she is wearing light-blue denim dungarees with a yellow T-shirt underneath. It's not the same uniform that everyone else has on. I wonder if she's some other pupil's sibling – maybe that is why she is also sitting alone.

If only she was the right type of person that my mam

would choose for me, but I know Mam will only select one of the other boys in the class. I have never felt a connection to boys. I am a boy, but I don't like boys (except for Simon) or doing boy things. Probably because I am afraid of men, especially the most important man in my life, my dad. That means I am not a 'normal' boy, which makes me a target for other boys and their brutality, who can sense my otherness and who don't like that. But thankfully, at three years old, this isn't a big problem for me yet.

I sit watching the girl's reflection for what feels like hours, but in reality, it's probably closer to two minutes. I work up the courage to turn away from the window to look at her directly, and even though I have turned from her reflection, there still seems to be a transparent glow surrounding her, like the light around her is refracting.

She is holding a pencil, and I sneak a look to see what she is drawing. It looks like a tree surrounded by grass and a river in the distance. My eyes flick back to her face, checking to see if I have been caught. She stops drawing and looks up at me. Even at three, experience tells me it's time to retreat and go back to staring out the window, but she doesn't let me go, she puts her hand on mine.

There is no weight to her hand, but I can feel her, and a spark of energy ignites the hairs on my skin; a tingle shoots from my toes to my head like someone is softly blowing on my neck. The picture she is drawing starts to come alive and the river begins to flow, the trees lean with the wind and the grass sways. All the colours from her drawing start to spill over the paper and onto the table, like a dam of coloured water bursting for freedom.

I am worried at first because this is the kind of thing my mam had warned me about; I was to sit still and wait for her to call me over, and definitely not make a friend without her official approval, nor get into any kind of trouble. Yet while the girl is holding my hand, I stop feeling worried, I'm free from anxiety about being the perfect child. I am paused in the moment.

She takes another pencil and writes something at the top of the picture.

G-I-S-E-L-L-E

I don't understand the word. I don't realise it's her name. And I don't know the effect these seven letters will have on the rest of my life.

My focus is broken when I hear my mam's voice. I look over at her standing beside a possible future new best friend she has targeted, a boy around the same age as me. He is dressed in slightly oversized Terenure College rugby kit, possibly his older brother's or maybe his own to grow into. I know that the fact that he is wearing a private school rugby kit would have been enough for my mam to single him out as a suitable friend candidate.

I turn back to Giselle, but she is gone, and with that my body becomes cold. There is no coloured water on the table, no river flowing; the glow from her bright white silhouette is now replaced by the dull yellow tint from the classroom lights. I think to myself that her mother must have come and got her while I was distracted.

Mam looks over at me and I can tell from her glare that she is already unimpressed by my actions as I sit alone, staring into vacant space, smiling to myself like I am in conversation with an old friend. But what was really happening was that I was witnessing the birth of a different world, the one that would ultimately save me, and I had just met the person to lead me through it. Yet to everyone else, I just look very peculiar. This, I am about to find out, is the problem with having invisible friends.

I get the nod from my mam to get up. It's time for me to play my part - there is only so much of this audition process that she can carry alone.

The small chair I am sitting on has metal legs and a wooden seat like a bowl holding me in place. I am not sure of the design theory behind it, but it seems to be the fashion of the time. Because I don't have long legs, I am not able to reach the floor when I am sitting in my bowl.

I swing my legs back and whip them forward to create enough momentum to lift my bum and thrust forward. I had practised this move many times when I would come with Mam to collect my brother from this very classroom.

I nail a perfect landing and glance over at Mam for approval, but she looks back at me with the kind of expression only a disappointed mother can cast. With just her eyes, she conveys that she isn't impressed, and that I am to join her straight away. So, I tuck my shirt in, pat down my jumper, pick my bag up and take a deep breath as I head into the eye of the storm; the hurricane of mothers standing together in a circle on their children's first day in a new school. I know it is only a matter of time before I am found out, when I let my mam down and fail to live up to the person she has been gloating about, the boy she has been describing as 'social, intelligent, sporty and a high achiever', despite the fact I am only three, and none of these things.

I look around the classroom hoping to catch another glimpse of Giselle. I want to feel her warmth again, to feel her connection so I can release the pressure of this intense moment and find an escape, but I can't find her. I look to the window. Maybe if I see my own reflection that will magic her back, and then we can get lost in her picture again.

I feel a tap on my shoulder.

I turn around so fast that my bag knocks into one of the mothers. I cringe, but I don't stop to apologise, my heart is pounding with excitement at the thought that this might be Giselle. But instead I see the boy in the rugby kit standing in front of me. My heartbeat slows, my excitement fades.

We both stand there, looking at each other, me wondering why he had tapped on my shoulder and he probably wondering why I turned around with such velocity. I hear my mam's voice above my head.

'Oh, Jonathan loves rugby.'

'Patrick plays for Terenure Juniors,' the boy's mam says.

They both look down at us, waiting for us to strike up what might be the friendship of a lifetime.

I don't know if it is the stress of the moment, but standing in front of Patrick, hearing my mam discussing me and my love for a sport I have no knowledge of or even interest in, knowing I will never be able to live up to her fantasy, my body chooses to express itself by letting go. And as the warm trickle of wee passes though the layers of my underwear and goes down my trousers, I mistake it for the same warm feeling I felt when Giselle held my hand only moments ago and when, for an instant, I had escaped.

Patrick is the first to notice. Being only three and lacking a filter to prevent him from expressing his internal thoughts, he points and says, 'wee wee', triggering a domino effect as each of the adults surrounding me starts to realise my predicament. I can feel every eyeball fixed on me. Every whisper of judgement is to my ears as loud as a roaring wind bashing against the wooden window frame of my bedroom. I am disgusting. I am a disappointment. I have let my mam down, and all her planning and networking, which was balancing on the edge of a cliff, has now crashed down to the sea with the reality of my being an outcast and an embarrassment.

Have you ever been in a moment where you witness something that your mind can't quite process? Time has a way of slowing down during these experiences, and that is what happens for me. While everyone is panicking about the boy who wet himself, I am looking past Patrick, past the adults and the other children playing, past the bookshelf towering at the back of the classroom, to a light that begins to emerge from the darkness in a corner.

It is Giselle.

I see the transparent glow as she materialises from behind the shadows and smiles at me. She isn't bothered by my situation, nor does she make me feel disappointed in myself. I want to escape with her, but I am trapped in the circle, trapped by these worldly anchors. If only I could exit my skin and float above everyone, exist as free-flowing energy on a cloud of white light as Giselle does, then I would be happy. I can feel my mam pulling me abruptly away from the circle, and from my fantasy, without sympathy. I don't want to turn away from Giselle – the last time I did she disappeared.

The school bell rings. My audition is over.

We leave the classroom. I've lost sight of Giselle again. I'm walking slightly behind my mam, using her body to conceal my wet trousers from the other children as we leave. I am trying to keep my legs straight with each step, a technique I developed to keep the wet material away from my skin; this wasn't my first public wetting.

My mam never held my hand as a child, I'm not sure why, and today is just the same. Maybe her own disconnected emotional experience as a child has affected her in a way she is unaware of. Maybe she needs an invisible friend but has never met the right one.

Me? Although I failed in joining the herd and in creating a special connection with my nominated male friend, I leave the school that day with the friend my mam would never have chosen for me. She isn't from the right family, she doesn't go to the right school, she isn't a boy. I know instinctively that she isn't even 'real', as nobody else can see her. But she is *my* choice.

We're standing outside the school now, watching the lollipop lady walk out into the traffic to let the groups of children and adults that have been building up on either side of the road get across. As we wait for our turn, I feel a gentle tingle run down my back, and then a delicate hand clutches my own.

I think Giselle is coming home with me.

CHAPTER 2

Learning How to Disappear

1984 (age four)

'Good morning, Giselle,' I say, as I lie in bed, eyes open and covers pulled up to just under my chin.

Beside me are Lambsy and Rabbit, my favourite soft toys that I sleep with every night. My grandmother on my father's side, who I called Grandma, had tailored clothes for both of them – she used to work as a seamstress. Lambsy wears a blue T-shirt and tiny matching shorts, and Rabbit has a green T-shirt with a brown checked shirt. I keep them both wrapped in the white knitted blanket I was baptised in, tucked beside me at night or resting on my pillow during the day. The blanket was made for me by my grandmother on my mam's side, who I call Mamo, as that is the Irish for grandmother.

I share this bedroom with Simon and Ruth, while Leah, who is still very little, gets to sleep with our parents. There was a time when I was the youngest and received all the benefits that came with that position in the family, but now I have been banished to the second-youngest position and all my perks have been revoked. Ruth and Simon are the first-born son and daughter, so they can enjoy the privileges that come with that, and Leah, being the youngest, is the most spoilt, and then there is me. I am not first of anything, or even the last now, I am just me, so I get overlooked a lot.

But now I have my new friend.

It's her first morning waking up with me in my house. For the first few months after she followed me home, she would only visit me for short periods. But lately she has started to spend more and more time with me, and last night I was feeling a little worried because Mam and Dad were fighting, so she decided to stay for a sleepover. I will need to show her around my room and introduce her to all my toys. I've never had a friend stay over before, so this is very exciting.

'Who are you talking to?' asks Ruth.

I hadn't realised I had greeted Giselle out loud. Usually I talk to her in my head.

'No one,' I say. I know there is no point explaining.

She doesn't seem impressed with my answer.

'Stop being such a weirdo,' she says.

Ruth gets out of bed and goes over to the small electric heater, and with a sense of entitlement only reserved for first-born children, she announces:

'I'm going first, you can wait in bed.'

We don't have central heating in our house, and Ireland isn't a very warm country, but we do have that heater. It is expensive to run, so we have developed a system: we get one minute each to stand in front of the warm blowing air while getting dressed. The aim is always to try to capture as much of the warmth as possible and if I'm lucky I am able to trap some of it inside my clothes to tide me over until I get to school, where the heating is always on.

Ruth is almost dressed when Simon jumps out of the bed and pushes her to the side to begin the hurried process of putting his uniform on.

'I wasn't finished,' Ruth protests, standing barefoot on the cold wooden floorboards beyond the reach of the warm air.

'That was one minute, I was counting', says Simon as he quickly buttons up his shirt.

'I'm telling Mam!' shouts Ruth. 'Mam, Simon won't let me use the heater!'

'I am,' he shouts back. 'She used her time up!'

Annoyed by the cacophony, my dad comes into the room and pulls out the plug on the heater.

'If you can't get dressed quietly, without fighting, then I am not paying for the heater anymore.' He picks up the contraption and leaves the room.

'I was dressed anyway,' chuckles Simon.

'Yeah, me too,' laughs Ruth.

They leave the room, heading for the kitchen to enjoy breakfast wearing their warm clothes.

I pull off my covers and step onto the floor. The wooden boards don't feel as cold as the heads of the nails that protrude from them. I make a mental note to try to avoid the cold metal as I walk over to get my uniform. There is a pile of clothes on top of a chair, and I need to find my white shirt, red jumper, dicky bow and trousers.

'Is this what you want to wear?' asks Giselle, inspecting my school outfit.

'No,' I answer, 'but it's what I'm told to wear.'

Giselle walks over to the cupboard where Ruth's clothes are hanging.

'I like this,' she says, holding up a white dress with a red heart pattern. 'Let's try this one on.'

'I'm only supposed to wear my uniform,' I say, but at the

same time I find myself walking over and taking the dress from her.

'Just for fun, come on,' insists Giselle. 'I want to see what this looks like on me.' I like how she talks about us like we're one and the same, which we are. I understand that.

I know I shouldn't try the dress on, as boys are not allowed to wear dresses, but Giselle really wants to see it on.

'Okay, just for you.'

I take off my pyjamas, and as the cold air from the draughty window rushes over my body, I step into the dress and pull it up until the straps are over my shoulders. Giselle claps in delight.

'You look so pretty,' she says as we look at ourselves in the small, cracked mirror leaning against the wall.

And as we stand, shivering in the middle of the room, I feel a warmth creeping over me. I turn to see if the heater has returned and is somehow softly blowing hot air my way, but there is just an empty space.

'Let me show you something,' Giselle says.

She raises her hands up as if she is slowly dancing. Her movements transform this dark space into a new world. She has opened a door to somewhere I have only glimpsed once before on the trial day at Presentation, when we first met. I have never been here and yet it feels like home, it feels like a place where I belong.

'What is this? Where are we?' I ask as I realise I am standing in a forest, surrounded by tall trees, my face bathed in the sunlight peeping through the clouds. Yet, at the same time, I am still standing in my bedroom, cold to the touch; it's almost like every time I blink, I am transported from my bedroom to this forest. I become absent in one world only to become present in the other.

And then Giselle tells me: 'We're in Domdie. Where we go whenever we need to disappear.'

'What do you mean?' I ask, still looking in the mirror at our reflection.

My concentration is broken by the sound of a heavy tread, rapidly making its way up the stairs to my room. I panic because I know if I get caught wearing my sister's dress I will be in trouble. I pull the straps down and jump out of the dress.

'Are you just getting out of bed now?' yells my dad from the other side of the door. Luckily, he has not come in and seen me in the dress. It's better to be punished for getting out of bed late rather than for the shameful act I have just performed.

'Sorry,' I say. 'It . . . it was an accident.' And I reach for my school uniform.

'You will have to go without breakfast now, there isn't enough time,' he says angrily as I hear him walking off.

The trousers I put on don't feel the same way the dress did. Pulling the shirt round my body doesn't feel right either.

'What is wrong with me?' I say out loud.

'Nothing,' replies Giselle. 'We are not wrong.' She hands me a pair of my sister's white socks. They're different to mine because they have a little motif at the bottom of the ankle.

'These aren't mine,' I say.

'Wear them for me,' she says simply.

I put them on, trying to ensure the motif is hidden away. It is only slightly visible above my leather shoe. It's funny how even this tiny design can cause so much controversy.

I go to the kitchen just as everyone is leaving, and as per my dad's instruction I don't get to have breakfast. We walk together down Fortfield Road, making a left onto Greenlea Road and then finally turning right onto Terenure Road West, where Presentation is situated.

I arrive at my classroom and greet my teacher, Mrs O'Shea.

'Good morning, Jonathan,' she says back to me. 'Please take your seat, you can read or play with Grace until everyone else arrives.'

I wander over to my table where Grace, my desk partner, is already sitting, and I put my bag down. Then I remember the socks, I still have them on, and I am at school. What if someone notices and calls my parents, I will be in so much trouble! Why did I listen to Giselle?

Grace and I have been sitting together since school started. I was supposed to be at the next table, beside Seán, but on the first day when we were being assigned our seating I managed to move my name beside Grace's.

Grace leans down to take a book out of her bag and puts it between us. Most mornings we read or colour a book together until the lessons starts.

'I like your socks,' she says.

'Thanks,' I reply nervously. 'I think I put them on by mistake,' I add quickly.

'They're the same as mine,' she says as she lifts her leg up, revealing her own socks. 'We can be sock friends.'

I pretend to be cool about this.

'Oh yeah, you're right, I do kinda like them, I suppose.'

'They suit you,' she says as she smiles at me.

Across the room I can see Giselle, smiling at me too. She and I are both happy that Grace didn't get angry with me and tell me I was a weirdo, she didn't even care that I wasn't supposed to be wearing them. I think I like Grace even more now. Maybe I will wear the socks again tomorrow.

CHAPTER 3

My Last Happy Moment

1984 (age four)

It's a dark and rainy October morning, but that isn't affecting my mood. My hair is a bit damp from not wearing my hood properly, and my uniform trousers are covered in wet patches because I enjoy jumping in every puddle we pass on the way to school on days like these.

I make my way to my classroom table and slowly slide my slightly damp bum in the chair. Halloween is only two weeks away so it's time to start constructing our costumes. My mam usually decides what I'll go as, but now I am old enough to choose what I want, and Giselle and I already have a plan.

Grace is looking forward to Halloween just as much as I am.

'What are you going as?' she asks me.

'A witch,' I say excitedly.

You see, for one night of the year I can wear a dress in public and nobody will have a problem with it. I think it's only fair that Giselle gets to dress me sometimes, like she did that morning when I tried on Ruth's white dress. But if my dad ever sees me wearing girls' clothes, he gets angry, so I hide myself. But not on Halloween.

'Me too, but a nice witch,' she states. 'A pink and purple pretty witch.'

She shows me her coloured paper supplies that her mam has packed for her.

'I'm going to be an evil witch,' I tell her. 'I'd like to be a pretty witch too, but I only have this . . .'

I pull out a black bin liner from my school bag.

Every year my costume is made from a black plastic bin bag. It's cost-effective and extremely handy, says my mam. Cutting a hole for your head at the top gives you a versatile template for almost any costume: last year I was a robot, which was achieved by adding some tinfoil (I was told to be careful, so that the foil could be taken off and reused for cooking later). I am too young to remember my previous costumes, but apparently the year before that I was a baby vampire. I'm a bit suspicious of that one: when I ask for more details to ensure my witch won't look anything like the baby vampire, I am greeted with a lot of vague information. I'm also puzzled by the notion of baby vampires.

'Do vampires have babies?' I ask Mam to better understand my past character.

'Of course they do,' she replies while peeling a potato for shepherd's pie.

This is one of my mam's regular dishes. Hers consists of 95 per cent potato, 3 per cent meat, 2 per cent peas and some water. As a result, the likelihood of getting any meat is slim. And unless you manage to get some of the liquid, you end up with a plate of mostly dry potato. Wasting food is not tolerated in our house, so you must sit at the table until you eat everything on your plate. Sometimes that can take hours because it's hard to swallow, and the longer you sit there, the colder and even less palatable the food gets (even though it wasn't all that tasty to begin with). But there is no getting away with leaving before you're done.

Sometimes I throw the remains of my dinner into the large plant pots my dad placed around the room. They are perfect for hiding unwanted food. I am always worried that the bits of foul-tasting mash will turn into seeds, and then a dinner plant will grow and we will end up having to eat even more of this tasteless food.

I wish we could have pasta, but for some unknown reason my mam does not like pasta. She sees it as a strange foreign food that mustn't be served in her home, unless it's prepared the way my dad makes it, as a form of dessert. He pours a full pack into a pressure cooker, adds milk, raisins and sugar, boils it for about thirty minutes and fills our bowls. We all love it and call it 'shells'.

My dad also cuts up apples from our garden, coats them in batter and deep-fries them in the chip pan. Even on our limited food budget he has a way of making something delicious. But as he is always out at work, we don't often get these treats.

I watch my mother put the potatoes in a saucepan full of cold water. I want to know more about baby vampires.

'But how do they have babies?' I ask. 'Don't they eat people? Wouldn't they eat their babies?' I'm pondering the idea of a parent eating their own baby.

But Mam has no more answers for me, and as she's beginning to look a little annoyed with my questioning, I go outside to the garden to find my dad. He is digging the beginnings of a pond. Dad is always starting a project, but then gets Simon and me to finish it. We ended up doing all the work on this pond for years after, and then we dug a second pond further down the garden. He uses us as his labour force, but at least we learn some useful skills along the way.

In between him slicing the soil with his spade, I manage to get his attention.

'Remember when I was a baby vampire at Halloween?' I ask him.

'No,' he replies with a confused look on his face.

'Mam said I was.'

'Oh yeah, last year, right, you looked great.' He smiles, like he is remembering the very moment.

'I was a robot last year,' I correct him.

His smile disappears, and he turns back to his spade. I guess that's as much information as I will be getting from him. I have no evidence to prove I was ever a baby vampire, but also nothing to suggest otherwise, so I will just have to trust my parents.

I'm very excited about another Halloween tradition, particular to Ireland: barmbrack, a quick bread, sweeter than sandwich bread, but not as rich as cake, with sultanas and raisins added in that have been soaked overnight in cold tea.

But it isn't just the taste that I love, it's the fact that hiding inside the fruit loaf is a surprise. A fortune-telling kind of surprise. These are the things that were typically hidden inside and what they predicted:

a pea: you will not marry that year

a matchstick: you will have an unhappy marriage

a piece of cloth or rag: you will have bad luck

a coin: you will enjoy good fortune

a ring: you will be wedded within the year

a bean: you will have a future without money

Nowadays, due to health reasons, of course, a shop-bought barmbrack only has a toy ring inside it. One year when a manufacturer inserted a real gold ring as a promotional ruse, the whole country went mad buying buns.

Mam made most of our 'bracks' to save money, and sometimes we would find a 10p coin wrapped in paper. Once Simon found a 50p coin, which we spent on two 25p rockets from the vegetable man who sold his goods from a van.

The best thing about the vegetable man and his mysterious van was that during October he would also sell fireworks. Fireworks are illegal in Ireland so unless you made the trip up to Northern Ireland and risked getting caught by either the Gardai on your way back into the Republic or, even worse, the British Army at a checkpoint inside Northern Ireland, this was the only way to get hold of fireworks. In my imagination, the vegetable man had special permission from both countries to allow him to travel over the border with a van full of fireworks to provide happiness to the children of the Republic.

He sold us little yellow rockets, and every now and then we got a dud that didn't take off, but we found use for those. Dad would regularly light a bonfire at the end of our garden to dispose of anything that didn't fit in the bin. Simon and I would throw in the broken rockets, and they would explode, and we would applaud. We also melted anything plastic we could find, tying the item to the end of a stick and holding it over the fire. As soon as the plastic started to drip, we would withdraw it from the heat and pretend it was a fighter plane, making it dive bomb over the annoying nettles that had wronged us in the past. As the melted plastic hit the leaf, the moisture from the plant would instantly cool the smouldering drips and let out a hiss, which added to the thrill.

Back in the classroom, I have also brought a plastic gold-painted ring, which I found in the middle of a brack my mum exceptionally bought for me from a shop. At Little Lunch – the fifteen-minute break in the morning before Big Lunch (which is thirty minutes and in the middle of the day), Ciara, Grace, Jemma, Louise, and I meet up in the playground as we always do. Usually at Little Lunch I would eat not only the Tracker bar my mam has packed for me for that time in the day, but also the rest of my packed lunch: a yogurt, a Capri Sun and a ham sandwich. But today there is no time to eat, as we need to find out if anyone got a golden ring and whether there will be a wedding to plan.

Crowding around in a circle, we take turns showing off our haul of monkey nuts and fruit, which we've each managed to pinch from home before trick or treat night. Those are the treats you usually get when you go from house to house on the big night, but if you're a bit strategic you know the good houses in the neighbourhood that gave away chocolate the year before. You prioritise those, and then you move on to the houses that offer the standard fruit and nuts. My house is on the bad list as we only offer the standard fare, whereas the Murphys, who live next door, always have a selection of fun-size chocolates – and once I saw someone leave holding a full-size Twix.

After we've munched on a few nuts, Ciara pulls out a plastic golden ring. We all gasp in shock. She turns to me and puts it on my finger.

'We're married now,' she says.

And then before I have time to respond, Grace puts another golden ring on my other finger.

'We're also married,' she says, with a shy smile.

'Thank you,' I say, slightly embarrassed but also enjoying the attention.

And then Jemma and Louise at the same time both hold out gold rings.

'Will you marry us too?' they ask together.

'What is going on?' I ask, confused as to how this has happened.

'It was Grace's idea,' says Jemma.

'I got a ring a few days ago and I told Jemma, who told me Louise got one too, and we both wanted to give them to you,' explains Grace.

And then Ciara chimes in. 'And Jemma and I got rings too, so we thought, let's all get married together.'

So, with my fingers heavy with golden rings, we all run around the playground taking turns to act out our weddings, and with each 'I do', I receive a kiss on my cheek, until the bell goes and everyone troops back inside.

I hold back for a moment and let everyone re-enter the classroom before I turn to Giselle.

'I kept this one for you,' I say as I reach into my pocket and take the ring I found in the brack the night before and hand it to her. 'Will you marry me?' I ask.

'I thought you'd never ask,' replies Giselle and then she kisses me on the cheek. 'I do forever.'

Those three years at Presentation were the happiest years

of my childhood. Throughout it all, I had this group of girl friends with whom I was very close and could always be myself around, not that all their parents understood how a boy could be their best friend (I missed out on a lot of parties). I felt connected and excited to be part of this world. We had so much fun together, playing hopscotch and hand-slapping games. I would always let myself get caught by the girls I liked the most during kiss-chase. We started a 'fancy paper club', collecting the perfumed papers that came in packages taped to the outside of girls' magazines. I never had the courage to buy one myself, nor was I ever offered one – I was only allowed to pick something from the comic shelf like *The Dandy*, *Beano* and *Whizzer and Chips*. I knew that the shelf with the *Bunty*, *Mandy*, *Jinty* and *Tammy* magazines was off limits, so I always picked *The Beano*. So when it came to showing off our fancy paper collections, I would inevitably have the smallest amount, usually given to me by my friends.

We teamed up together for our mandatory Irish dancing and Irish language classes, which we had to take to keep our heritage alive. My mam spoke Irish with her parents so I should have been fluent, but because of her lifelong dispute with Mamo, her mam, who had only spoken Irish to her kids, she made a point of only speaking English to me and my siblings. It was an act of rebellion towards Mamo but also a way of making sure we'd not feel socially and culturally disconnected, the way she had felt throughout her childhood.

During the dance lessons, we all piled into the small barn next to the school and the boys would line up on one side of the hall and the girls on the other. A local man would come in to play his accordion for us and we would dance to his music.

The girls would start by dancing in the middle, and then the boys would dance up to join them. Most of the boys were embarrassed at taking part, but I felt a kind of freedom when I danced. It was almost like being in Domdie, the parallel world Giselle takes me to whenever things get too much for me, while at the same time being present in this world too. There was something about music and how it entered my body, how it vibrated inside me, that I loved. I'd allow my body the freedom to move however it felt and if anyone saw me, they wouldn't think I was being strange, I was just doing my dance lesson.

The only time I wasn't with my friends was for one hour each day, when I was taken out of class to a tiny room a few doors down. There were just three other kids with me during these lessons. I had overheard my mam talking to my teacher about me falling behind and daydreaming too much, and as her hopes and dreams had been set on me attending Terenure College, alongside Patrick and all the other well-to-do boys in my class, I was now sitting for one hour a day away from my friends, trying to catch up.

But that didn't bother me. I had real friends that I identified with, I felt connected and excited to be part of this world. When I was not in school, I would usually be hanging out in Laverna, which was the common grass expanse around the corner from our house, sometimes talking to Giselle in my head, off on an adventure with Simon and his friends on our bikes in Lakelands, which was a small, wooded area at the back of Terenure College.

And then it all started going downhill.

CHAPTER 4

An Enemy Rises

1984 (age four)

I am sitting in the front seat of my mam's car. I have the window down, and I'm letting the wind envelop my face and drown out the unwelcome noise this world is so full of.

We are slowing down and as the lights change from green to orange and then to red, Mam puts her arm across my chest so that I don't fall forward. She always does this when she brakes. Maybe someone should invent a better way to hold people in place, when sitting in their car seats. That physical touch between me and her feels so unusual to me.

'Why doesn't she ever hold me without a reason?' I ask Giselle, who is sitting beside me.

We both fit on the large front seat, as it is clearly designed for a full-sized adult. It helps that I am sitting on the far edge, as close to the window as possible, creating even more space for her, in the same way I share my life with her.

'We have each other for that,' replies Giselle.

I'd like to think my mam loves me, but she isn't very good at showing it. I often see other mams at school embracing their sons and daughters, or pushing them on a swing, holding their hands and hugging them for no reason. But as I said, mine had a plan for me, and that plan didn't prioritise emotional care. Emotions were deemed to be a weakness, and I was not to be weak. I know now that her intention was good, but her method was harsh for a young child like me.

If I disobey my mam and she wants to punish me, she tells me how the Bold Boys' School van will wait for me outside or will come for me while I sleep. Then it will take me away to the school for bold boys ('bold' in Irish means 'naughty'). I hide under the bed, watching the door, terrified of its imminent arrival. Sometimes, to really give us a fright, my mam takes us kids out of our beds and puts us outside the front door in the middle of the night to be collected. We sit there in the dark, shivering in just our underpants, watching the road in anticipation of the van pulling up.

Mam had threatened me with this so many times, that it became an anxiety that I took to bed with me. For years, I would sleep so lightly because of it, but also because of the alarm I wore on my pyjamas to alert me when I wet the bed. It was a small box that fitted on my waistband with a large safety pin, with a sensor that was set inside my underwear. If the pad got wet, the alarm went off, and my anxiety about that was only made worse by the fear of my parents' anger when it went off.

We have stopped beside a few small shops at an intersection called Kimmage Crossroads, also known as the KCR. At the heart of the KCR is a petrol station, which doubles as a small independent video rental shop which we are members of, and is aptly named 'Crossroads'. They had a second branch about five minutes away in Crumlin. This shop was not at a crossroads, but it was also called Crossroads, confusingly.

My school peers would talk about videos they rented from Xtravision, the big premium video rental chain in Ireland. Patrick always managed to get the newest movie releases there, and I would end up pretending I had seen them too. I guess because of Mam I needed to impress him and pretend I was on his level. I also became very good at guessing the plot of a film, based on its title.

The Crossroads shop is always in semi-darkness, with wall-to-wall videos and outdated cardboard cut-outs in each corner. The air is filled with an aroma of popcorn and petrol and somehow, they go well together.

Scattered throughout the shop floor are large metal baskets filled with unpopular releases that are half-price. Because the shop is so small, there is only ever one copy of each new release, unlike Xtravision. You can pre-book one by writing your name and address in a black book on the counter, but most of the time, if someone else sees the video lying in the return pile, they pull it out and rent it then and there, and no-one checks the list to see if it's been pre-booked. It's quite chaotic.

Often, we took a video home, only to realise we had the wrong movie, because all the videos looked the same piled behind the shop counter in their generic plastic cases. The promo boxes they came in were only used for display. All it took was for the shop attendant to be distracted for a moment, and they put the wrong video into your box.

It was not always a bad thing. Once we rented *The Muppets Take Manhattan*, but when we pressed play, it was a movie called *Tron*. Ruth wasn't too impressed, but Simon and I loved it.

Leaning out of the window while stopped at the lights, I am watching several people going in and out of Crossroads and the newsagent. I can't help but imagine what their life is like. Who are they? Where do they live? Are they returning a late video? The traffic lights turn green and, acting like there

JONATHAN JOLY

is a time limit on how long you can remain stationary, Mam slams down the accelerator and off the car screeches.

We pull into Sundrive Shopping Centre, which has at its core a large Superquinn, an Irish supermarket chain. In the middle of the square-shaped enclosure is a small parking area, and because we come here often, my mam has become very good at finding a spot, despite the limited number of spaces. Parking to her is a competitive sport and she is a competitive person. As she waits, her ears are tuned for the clashing sound of a returned trolley. She spots her mark and observes them carefully to try to predict their route to their car before another predator swoops in before her.

Once the parked car is identified she pulls up in front of it, puts on her indicator and waits. You can see the driver's mounting panic as Mam fixes her eyes on them, giving out strong signals that something bad might happen if they don't vacate with haste.

This time is no different. Her target is a middle-aged woman, and Mam is staring at her. The woman looks very scared.

'I know I am slightly afraid of Mam sometimes,' I whisper to Giselle. 'But why is someone who doesn't know her afraid?'

'She never gets cross with us when we are outside of the house, but maybe other people know what she is like at home?' replies Giselle.

'Maybe getting cross is only for us when we're at home, and for everyone else when out in public?'

'I'm scared of her all the time,' says Giselle.

Suddenly, the woman drops a full bag of shopping as she panics, and a bottle of milk rolls quickly away across the car park and crashes against a pillar. The vision of white liquid exploding across the grey concrete is like something you would see on television.

'Oh, for God's sake,' Mam cries out, knowing this will lengthen the process considerably. She gives up on this space and moves on.

When we eventually find a parking space and get out of the car, I notice the play bus parked out front. It's a tired-looking coach that looks like it was once used for regular national travel, but it's now been converted into a crèche for parents who don't want to take their kids into the shopping centre. It's like a dedicated children's waiting area, full of art supplies, books and toys. I love that place, but sadly it isn't free and things that aren't free are usually not for me.

We don't often go on a shopping trip like this, as most of the food we eat is either delivered by the local vegetable man – the one who sold fireworks in October – or direct from a farm. So whenever we come here, there is always a glimmer of hope that Mam will be in a good enough mood to leave me at the crèche.

'Can I wait for you on the bus?' I ask Mam, with little hope as we approach it.

'It's one pound, Jonathan,' she replies sternly.

'Fine,' I say in a sad voice, hoping my downbeat tone will make her think again. It's a strategy that rarely works.

We head over to the small wooden shed next to the shop door. This means Mam is planning on collecting a trolley, and that this is going to be a long shop.

'We need to get on the bus, Giselle,' I say.

We walk together behind Mam, dragging our feet, acting up slightly, hoping that will convince her that putting me on the bus is the best solution for everyone. It's a thin line though, which will either result in punishment or victory.

'Let's be less nice to go shopping with,' Giselle advises.

'I know,' I reply. 'I am trying.'

'Do you want to grab the trolley, Jonathan?' Mam asks as she unfolds her long shopping list.

There are two types of trollies in the bay and I know she wants the larger, so I deliberately grab the smaller one to see where that gets me.

'I got it,' I say as I wheel over the wrong trolley.

'What are you messing at, you know that's the wrong one,' she says, visibly annoyed.

'You said get the trolley, you didn't say which one,' I retort.

'You're just like your father, you never listen,' she mumbles as she grabs the trolley from me and wheels it back over to the bay.

I wander over to the charity box in the shape of a large dog that I like to talk to whenever I see it. It has an opening at the top of his head to place coins into. I never put anything in but always wonder what the dog would do if I did. Would he bark, or wag his tail? I always give the dog a hug, as its size is just right for me. Since I barely get hugs at home – only when Dad feels guilty after shouting at me – but see hugs happen to other people in person and on television, I take the opportunity to experience an embrace when I can get it, even if it's with a large dog-shaped lump of plastic outside a supermarket.

'When we grow up, we're going to have loads of dogs,' I announce to Giselle, with confidence, like this is a matter of fact.

'A real dog might even hug us back too,' she says.

I don't notice Mam has collected a trolley and entered the shop, assuming I am following her. When she realises that I am not, she comes back outside to find me hugging the large plastic dog.

'What are you doing?' she asks. 'I can't keep my eyes on you all the time, Jonathan, you need to pay attention and stop wandering off like this.'

'Sorry,' I say, eyes pointed down to show how apologetic I am.

She sighs.

'Right, let's put you on the bus,' she says.

I smile and look over at Giselle, keeping my grin to a minimum, not showing my excitement. It's best to make it look like this is all Mam's idea. We walk over to the bus and Mam knocks on the plastic window to get the attention of the driver so that he lets us in.

'Hi, just one please,' she says to the man, as she reaches into her purse to find a one-pound note. The green paper currency is larger than the palm of my hand and has a picture of a sad lady who looks like she just got out of a shower and has a towel wrapped around her. The back of the banknote looks like a child has written all over it with dark green and light red markers, mixing them together to make a reddish brown.

In her purse, there is also a five-pound note, which has a nun on it, and a ten-pound note with a man with long curly hair. I always wonder how he gets away with having such long, pretty hair when he is a man. Clearly it doesn't seem to bother anyone. Yet if I were to ever suggest that I wanted to grow my hair long like his, I would be told that boys don't have long hair.

Giselle always manages to go places with me for free, which I am grateful for, because I don't like being away from her, and I am certain that if Mam had to pay another pound for her, she would never go anywhere with me.

'I won't be long, okay?' she says as I climb aboard. She leaves before she tells the driver my name, so I am left to attend to the admin on my own.

'What's your name, son,' asks the driver.

'Jonathan,' I reply, a little unsure of myself talking to a strange man.

'Okay, John, take a seat,' he says as he places a sticker with the name 'John' on my jumper. I think about correcting him – I am not called John, that's my father's name – but I don't have the confidence, and no matter how much Giselle tries to tell him, he can't see or hear her, so I make my way down the bus, wearing a badge with the wrong name.

An hour later Mam has finished her shopping, and after she fills the car with all the shopping bags, she collects me, and we drive off.

'Don't tell your father that I let you go on the bus,' she says as we make our way home.

'I won't,' I reply, looking out the window. I know that he won't approve of the money spent.

We pull into the driveway just as Dad is coming out of the

front door. I can tell from the change in my mam's energy that there is something wrong. He comes straight over to her side of the car and they begin arguing about something through the window, so I open my door and quietly climb out. I don't want to draw attention to myself and become part of this drama.

As I close the door, it makes a loud clunk and suddenly I am in focus.

'Don't slam the fucking door, you idiot,' Dad says as he walks around the car to me. I freeze in fear, and he comes closer.

'How many fucking times do I have to keep saying the same things to you, you never listen, do you? You're just like your mother,' he says, echoing what she said about him only a few hours ago.

My parents have always fought, it is something that Ruth, Simon, Leah and I are all used to as this point, as if it is just the norm. I assume everyone else's parents are the same. But recently, the fighting has started to involve us kids. Whenever my parents get angry now and start throwing cups and plates at each other, they also turn to whichever one of us is nearby, and pick on us. We become the outlet for their frustration and rage. It's almost as if they can never resolve their own issues, so they pick on people they can win fights with.

'I don't want to marry someone if I have to fight with them all the time,' I say to Giselle.

'And we don't want our kids to be afraid of us either,' she adds. As he towers over me, Dad notices I am wearing the sticker with his name on it that my mother and I had forgotten to take off.

'I thought I told you not to let him on that fucking bus!' he shouts as he rips my sticker off. I am beginning to panic, so I run into the house, but he follows me.

'Don't you run away from me when I am talking to you,' he says, as he follows me into my bedroom. He is angrier than before, something in him has snapped.

He has a look in his eye of hate, anger and pain. He steps closer, and a darkness fills the room as his shadow engulfs me. I can feel my small child's body become even smaller. I look for Giselle, but she has gone.

I am looking at Dad, trying to remember all the fun times we had together, trying to forget this moment as it plays out in real time. I want it to be Mam and Dad fighting, and not Dad and me. But the father who can be loving seems to have been replaced by what I can only describe as an enemy. He is so powerful that he has scared away my invisible friend.

I begin to cry as he moves closer to me, and then from behind I hear a voice. It's Simon, who has come to help me.

The Enemy turns around and looks at Simon as he stands there, ready to try to save his little brother, only a child himself but willing to make the sacrifice because he feels a responsibility, being the older brother.

'Step one fucking foot into this room and I will kill you where you stand,' shouts the Enemy to Simon.

Simon just looks at me. I can see the distress in his eyes; he wants to protect me, but he can't. But his actions are enough to distract the Enemy and allow my father to resurface as the shadow of darkness retreats, and light begins to fill the room once more.

Dad pushes Simon and leaves the room. Seconds later, Mam shouts for us to come help her with the shopping, like nothing has happened.

But everything has happened. It was the first time I saw a side to Dad I never knew existed. And from that day, I was to see the Enemy a lot more often. Every time he shows up and attacks, moments later the dad I know returns and looks for forgiveness. He will force a hug out of me and say its Mam's fault. This is very confusing for me; it feels like I live with two dads. This split personality has taken a toll on me trusting people. How do I know there isn't a monster inside everyone?

I want to thank Simon for what he's just done, but because

we are told not to indulge in our emotions, I can't express myself with anyone other than Giselle.

Thirty-seven years later, I can say this to Simon: you are the only person in this world that ever stood up for me and I will be forever thankful for that.

CHAPTER 5

London Respite

1985 (age five)

It's been almost a year since the first day the Enemy appeared, and life has become a lot darker. Mam and Dad's fights have become louder and more violent. At this rate I think we might run out of plates and cups soon, as they keep throwing them at the kitchen wall.

Thankfully, Giselle has started introducing me to other invisible friends in Domdie, but they don't talk to me. I see them, and because they are silent, it's a bit like they are extras in our movie, but just knowing they're there brings me comfort. I find myself spending more and more time with them, and less time interacting with the real world.

Mam has started to notice my disconnection. She gets frustrated by it. I did mention Giselle to her once, but she wasn't really listening. She thinks that I am daydreaming all the time, that I am too lost in my mind. She is worried that if I carry on like this, I won't make real friends that will help me climb the social ladder. She has started working again and travels a bit for her job as a swimming teacher trainer, and she has decided to take me away with her when she can, as she doesn't want to leave me at home with my dad. I like going places with my mam on my own. When you're the third child of four, getting alone time with your mother is always rare, so when it happens I relish the occasion.

One trip that year is particularly exciting, because it is to London. We set off in the car, hoping it won't rain all the way there. The Irish have an inextricably close relationship with rain, and we have particular ways of describing it. *Spitting rain* wouldn't stop you going for a walk or having a picnic on a freezing beach holiday in Mayo, but *wet rain* can sneak up on you. It presents itself as mist, but somehow soaks deep into your clothes and leaves you with a red face and runny nose. Neither requires an umbrella, however, that would be reserved for *pissing rain*. This is a heavy soaking and will make you rethink your plans to walk to school, but then you remember that you don't have any other way to get to school and on arrival, there is a small chance your wet clothes might earn you a day off.

Then we move into top-tier Irish rain: *bucketing* and *hooring*. Although each are similar in volume to *pissing rain*, the added element of directional wind has consequences. The very idea of leaving the house must be thoroughly questioned, unless you are on a caravan holiday in Wexford or stuck on a boat on the River Shannon, when not going to the local pub to pass the time isn't an option.

The rain that makes the Irish stay indoors is the *lashing* or *hammering* type. There isn't a setting on your car wipers for this: even when the wipers are thrashing from side to side at top speed, your visibility is zero, so you stay put.

Luckily, the sun is shining all the way to the coast and during the boat journey too.

'Have you ever been here before?' I ask Giselle, as the ferry door opens, and all the cars get ready to leave the ship.

'No,' says Giselle, 'I've only ever been where you have been.'

Mam turns the key and the car roars into life. Instead of RTÉ Radio 1, a loud static sound blares out from the radio, confirming that we are now in England, therefore no longer able to hear the radio station we were listening to before we boarded this ship.

'Are you ready?' Mam says. 'Your first time in another country.' She sounds happy for me.

As the car moves forward it slightly wobbles from side to

side because of the waves gently pushing the ship against the pier. Mam lines the car up in the queue to drive over the large metal bridge that has been lowered to let us onto land. As the wheels roll onto the bridge there is a loud crash, and for a moment I'm worried we won't make it to the new country after all, but then we are off the ship and driving on a road again.

'Welcome to England!' Mam says to me.

'Welcome to England!' I say to Giselle, joyfully.

'Well, technically we're in Wales,' Mam remarks, 'but we will be in England soon.'

'We're in a whale?' asks Giselle, nervously. 'Do you think you can drive into sharks, too?'

We approach the customs and passport control.

'Okay, Jonathan, no messing, all right?' Mam says firmly, knowing I am likely to say something wrong at a crucial moment.

She pulls up to a small wooden booth where a man is sat inside. He slides open his window as Mam begins the process of rolling down hers. Opening the window in a 1981 Ford Escort is an event; the first few revolutions of the handle result in nothing, and then on the fourth or fifth time the window starts to lower. It takes maybe a full minute for her to get it all the way down, and all this time the man is just sitting there and watching.

She leans out and hands him her passport.

'Do we not have a passport?' asks Giselle.

'No one ever asked me for one, so maybe I have special permission like the vegetable man has,' I reply quietly, making sure I don't draw attention to myself, as Mam instructed.

The officer is looking through the passport.

'Business or pleasure?' he asks, seeing what other stamps she has.

'Bit of both,' replies my mam. 'I'm a swimming teacher trainer, and I'm doing a class in London, but I've brought my son with me,' she says with obvious confidence and pride that she's a woman travelling for business.

My mam was not the type to just stay at home and be a housebound mother forever; she needed to have her own salary and wasn't happy living with the financial arrangement put in place by my father after she left her nursing job when she had me.

Most weeks he would forget to give her money to do the weekly food shop until she pestered him, and then finally at the end of the week he would give in. But then when she would come to him the following Monday for the food shop again, he would get annoyed. A few weeks ago, things had taken a turn for the worse.

'How have you spent that already?' he demanded angrily.

'It's the food for the family, we need it,' she replied.

'You need to budget better, Brid. In fact, I will do the shop from now on,' he said. 'You can just do the cooking and cleaning.'

Becoming dependent on someone else had been hard for her – now she was trapped and under his control. She had always been so proud of her old nursing job, and of having her independence. Before 1973, there had been a marriage bar in Ireland, which meant a woman could not work for a state employer after marriage. When that law was lifted, Mam became the only married nurse the hospital had ever had, and that was also something she was proud of.

But in 1979, just after Mam and Dad had moved into their new house, pregnant with me, and already having had two babies, she had ended her career as a full-time nurse in Temple Street and started a part-time job in another hospital called The Matter. She'd worked there until I was born.

Mam would tell me later that a few weeks after my arrival, Dad had been called into work. His office had only been a five-minute walk from Herbert Park in Ballsbridge, Dublin, so he'd left Mam with us three kids to wait for him by the River Dodder.

It was a warm March afternoon, which was a bit of a novelty for Ireland, so we were making the best of this cloudless sky, sitting outside without our coats on. Ruth was watching the ducks from the edge of the river and Simon was sitting next to me, while I was being fed by our mother. Ruth was able to walk but Simon was still only crawling, and I, well, I couldn't do much.

Suddenly, Ruth lost her balance and fell into the river. Mam screamed when she heard the terrifying sound – SPLASH! Ruth bobbed intermittently above and below the water surface. Mam jumped up from feeding me, placed me down beside Simon, and told him to look after me. I'm not sure he understood the gravity of the situation or the importance of his sudden role as my guardian, but neither did I; I was too busy wondering where my lunch had gone.

Mam rushed to the edge of the river to see Ruth being slowly carried away by the current and getting lost in the darkness of the water. There was no one else around to help her. She couldn't swim herself, so she couldn't just jump in and grab Ruth, because that would mean she would have to leave her two other babies alone by the side of the river, putting herself in danger and being no use to Ruth or herself.

With few options, she lay down at the river's edge and reached out to grab hold of Ruth, but Ruth kept moving further out from the riverbank.

Eventually she managed to hook one finger into Ruth's shoe and slowly pulled her in until she was able to get her hand over her leg and drag her out of the water.

The whole ordeal was over in minutes, but I'd imagine for my mam it lasted for ever. I'm sure she replayed this very event repeatedly, and I bet sometimes in her dreams she couldn't save Ruth, or maybe sometimes she did jump in, got herself lost in the dark waters and as she slowly sank, she looked up at her two baby boys alone, and wondered what would become of them.

But thankfully none of those nightmares was a reality, and we all made it home safely that day. I am sure I would have been fine either way, as my invisible friends were already looking out for me, I just didn't know it yet.

Prompted by this wake-up call, she and her friend Anya had signed up for swimming lessons at a nearby pool in Templogue a few weeks later. They had this deal with each other that once a year, they would sign up to learn a new skill. The previous year it had been ballroom dancing, so when it came to deciding what to do that year, Mam said, 'Let's learn to swim.' You have to understand that a lot of Irish people did not know how to swim back then, so it wasn't that unusual.

After a few lessons, she'd then signed up for Mam and baby

classes and brought all three of us with her to teach us how to swim, should we ever be in danger again.

Sometime later, Mam's swimming teacher Mr Brennan asked her, 'Have you thought about doing a lifesaving class? They're always looking for strong swimmers, and you seem very confident in the water.'

Mam took one look at us and turned back to Mr Brennan. 'I want to be able to save my babies, so yes, sign me up.'

She passed the course, and it was suggested by one of her friends that she should then learn to become a swimming teacher. She signed up for that and qualified shortly after. Then one day, while waiting for Ruth's swimming lesson to finish back in Templogue, she got talking to the manager of the pool, and when he heard she was a qualified teacher he offered her a job on the spot.

While she taught lessons, Simon and I would sit beside the pool where she could keep an eye on us. I was one at this stage and Simon was two. She continued her training and soon she was offered work from Northern Ireland, as she had no specific religion and wasn't known to anyone. This was an important aspect of the job as she was a Catholic woman from the Republic of Ireland who wouldn't have been welcome in certain areas in Northern Ireland, and might even have become a target herself. But Mam kept her mouth shut and continued to work without any issues and this then led to her getting a few days' work in London, which is why we'd taken the boat over.

At the border control, the man pauses and scans the car and me, before handing her back her passport and waving us through.

'That was a lot easier than crossing the border to go to Northern Ireland,' I say to Giselle. 'We didn't even have to get out of the car.'

It takes many hours to reach London, but once there it feels like it takes a lot longer to reach my mam's friend Mayra's place, driving all through the winding city streets.

'Is this the biggest city in the world?' asks Giselle.

We strain our necks looking up at the giant buildings that reach up into the sky. I've never seen anything like this in real life, only on television, as the tallest building in Dublin is Liberty Hall, which has seventeen floors, whereas right now we are driving past a building called Tower 42 which has forty-seven floors. Mam tells me that you could stack three of Ireland's tallest building on top and it would still be taller.

Mayra's house is probably the biggest I've ever been in; it even has a swimming pool in the garden. Inside the front door is a large winding staircase that reaches up four floors.

Everyone who lives here has their own bedroom and even bathroom. It's like a hotel, not that I have ever been to one, but this is what I imagine it's like.

Mayra has two children, a son and a daughter, and their bedrooms are like toy shops filled with everything I've ever wanted.

'Are we dreaming?' I ask Giselle. 'This is like a wonderland. They must be so happy, all the time.'

'Not necessarily,' says a voice from behind.

I quickly turn around to see a lady standing in front of me, dressed in a brown linen suit with what looks like a handkerchief wrapped over her head. I'm not sure if she is invisible or real, it is not always obvious which is which at first, but the fact that she remarked on my conversation with Giselle leads me to believe she is invisible.

'Do you live here?' I ask her.

'I live everywhere and nowhere,' she replies.

'Jonathan!' shouts my mam from downstairs, 'Your lunch is on the table.'

'Coming!' I shout back very loudly, so that she can hear me in this enormous house.

'You're not from around here, are you?' asks the strange woman.

'No,' I reply, 'I'm here with my mam.'

'And we drove in a whale!' shouts Giselle, excited to tell someone this fact.

I realise this woman is able to hear Giselle. I look a little more closely at her.

'Are you real?' I ask her.

'Are *you* real?' she snaps back at me.

It's a fair question, one I have to consider for a bit.

'I think I am, but normally people only I can see don't talk to me.'

'I have the opposite problem, no one ever listens to me,' says the woman, looking sad and dropping her guard.

'Maybe they just can't hear you,' I say, wanting to make her happy.

'Jonathan is the only one who can hear me,' Giselle explains. 'I've tried to talk to other people, but it's a waste of time, I think they are all too busy to hear us.'

'Well, thank you for hearing me,' the lady answers as she begins to walk down the hall. 'It's hard being in a crowded world when no one can hear you.'

And then she is gone.

'I guess sometimes the invisible need visible friends, just as much as we need them,' I say to Giselle. 'That was the first invisible person to talk to me, other than you. I didn't even know that was possible.'

'When we first met, you lived your life in silence,' explains Giselle. 'You connected with me, and you've been listening out for others like me ever since, without realising it.'

'Then why don't more of them talk to me?' I ask her.

'Because their message isn't for you,' she replies. 'It's for the people they are with who are not listening to them.'

I know what that feels like too, thinking about my own experience of not being heard or even seen by most people in my life.

Suddenly the lady is back.

'I remember what I wanted to say to you!' she exclaims. 'When I saw you, I could see the sadness you carry, and I wanted to tell you that you are surrounded by so much love, but you just can't see it because your parents argue all the time. You need to know, it's not your fault. They love you, I can see it.'

I'm so stunned by what she says, and by the mix of emotions I feel, that at first I don't say anything. And then, just as I'm about to thank her, I hear my mother's voice again.

'Jonathan! It's getting cold!' She sounds annoyed.

'If my dinner gets cold, that will be my fault, so I'd better go,' I say to the lady. 'But we can play later.'

When I arrive in the kitchen, there is a selection of food on display I've never seen before. In fact, every cupboard in this palace is filled with tasty treats and snacks. There is even a large red tin of assorted biscuits with 'Rover' written across the top, just resting on the table. In our house the most exciting thing you might find is a small packet of Custard Creams, or maybe Bunkbeds for a special occasion. Bunkbeds are an Irish delight, consisting of soft pink marshmallow sprinkled with coconut shavings on a crunchy biscuit base. They come stacked two-by-two inside a clear plastic package, that's why we call them bunkbeds.

While I am busy eating everything I can fit inside my small body, I am also listening to my mam talking about clingfilm with Mayra and her husband.

Mayra hands her a small box and says: 'Take this home, it's way better than the clingfilm method, and you don't need to present a marriage certificate here to get them either.'

I only realise years later that they are talking about condoms. At the time, contraception such as condoms was only available with a prescription from a doctor in Ireland, and you would also need to prove your marriage with a certificate and provide a good reason why you needed to prevent a pregnancy. This is probably why I am the third baby born to my mam, and all born within year of each other apart from Leah, who is three years younger than me, which might have something to do with the abundance of clingfilm in our house.

After lunch, we venture back into the city and visit a place called a cinema. They have them back home but I have never been to one. There is a new movie everyone is talking about called *The Goonies*, about a group of young misfits who discover an ancient map and set out on an adventure to find a legendary pirate's lost treasure. Being in a cinema is an amazing experience and I love being immersed in the film.

And then the following day, my mam takes me to another magical place called Hamleys, and tells me I can pick out a toy.

'How are we meant to pick a single toy here?' asks Giselle, looking around at the walls of toys.

And then I notice the sign for the stairs.

'There are four floors of toys!' I say, getting nervous that I will never be able to make a choice. But after only an hour and several denied options because of budget restrictions, I finally get approval on a little wooden train set that has four carriages that connect with magnets.

'Okay, shall we go?' says Mam, looking at her watch. 'That took longer than I expected.'

'It would have been faster if we had known the rules at the start, instead of telling us we could pick any toy,' says Giselle.

I laugh out loud at her response.

'What's so funny?' asks Mam as we leave the shop.

'Nothing,' I say, 'I was just thinking of something funny Grace said at school.'

The rest of my time in London is spent hanging out at the house while Mam is at work. Giselle and I pretend this is our house, and that this is our happy life together, away from our enemies, away from the shouting and the noise that causes us to escape to Domdie. We play with the lady, our new friend. She tells us about the connection she once had with someone who doesn't talk to her anymore. I tell her she could visit us in Ireland anytime she wants to, but I warn her about the Enemy. Giselle even invites her to Domdie and says she can stay there, and that she doesn't have to be on her own anymore.

It is fun having two invisible friends, but soon we are travelling back to Ireland, where reality is about to get a whole lot worse.

CHAPTER 6

Going to Hell and Making Another Friend

1985 (age five)

'Don't do it,' says Ruth. 'What if he appears?' she asks fearfully, but Simon wants to know if the rumours are true.

It's a cold overcast December morning, and Simon, Ruth and I are all sitting on a collection of large boulders next to the ruins of an imposing building, eating crisps. Leah, Mam and John (I just can't call him Dad anymore) are slowly making their way up the hill to join us, as we three had run ahead because of Mam and John's arguing. They started at breakfast and haven't stopped, and we don't want to become part of that drama. Baby Leah is attached to Mam in a baby sling, so unfortunately we had to leave her behind.

This is a typical Sunday morning for my family. It starts

with a row, and when neither side can win, we kids get pushed into the car and led up a mountain.

We usually end up at one of three locations on these days out: the powerful and impressive waterfall at Powerscourt, the endless, breathtaking mountains of Wicklow, or the hike up Killiney Hill, which ends with a stunning view over Dublin Bay. Sometimes if the weather is clear enough, you can see parts of England in the distance, or maybe it is just the clouds resting on the horizon. Either way, it is spectacular.

Today we are at the summit of Montpelier Hill in the Wicklow mountains. It's a relief to be here. It's only been a week since we returned home from London, and in that short space of time things have escalated between my parents. I know the lady from London told me this isn't my fault, but I keep hearing my name being shouted in anger, which is making me feel like it *is* all my fault. Perhaps if I were like the other boys at school, like Patrick or Seán, then maybe my parents wouldn't fight as much.

'Don't be a chicken,' says Simon.

'I'm not a chicken, I just don't want to get into trouble,' replies Ruth. 'Mam said to wait for her at the top, and not to wander off.'

'We are at the top, and we are not going to wander off,' he says, scornfully. 'Come on,' he repeats as he jumps down from the large boulder he is sitting on, taking care not to spill his crisps.

He turns to me. 'Flynner, you coming?'

Simon and Ruth call me 'Flynner' because Mam told them that when I was born, I was little Johnny Flynn from the nursery rhyme, and it just stuck. My other nickname in the family is 'The Reactor' because I get very upset and react all the time to the smallest of things. I am sure I am difficult sometimes, but I don't know how to control my emotions, or Giselle's for that matter.

'You don't have to go with him just because he asked you to,' announces Ruth, being the eldest, and looking out for me, I think.

'Should we go with Simon?' I ask Giselle, looking from Ruth to Simon, trying to decide. 'Or should we stay with Ruth?'

'Do you think Ruth wants us to stay with her because she is worried about us, or because she doesn't want to be left alone?' asks Giselle.

'Well, I'm going with or without you chickens.' Simon finishes his packet of crisps and begins to walk over to the main entrance of the burnt-out ruins.

'Wait!' I shout. 'I'm coming too!' I might as well join him because I am curious. Also, I've finished my crisps.

'You can't leave me here on my own, guys!' Ruth cries out.

'Then come with us,' shouts Simon over his shoulder as he forges ahead.

Ruth joins me and we try to catch up with Simon. But we are wearing our heavy green rubber wellies that are hard to walk in. Mam never lets us wear trainers on a hike even though it makes more sense to me because there is always so much more running involved than jumping in puddles. But she never listens.

'You go in first, Flynner,' says Simon, as we stand at the door of the house.

I don't know why I always do these stupid things whenever I am told, I guess as the third child I am always happy on the rare occasion I get to be the centre of attention. I peer into the spooky dark ruins, but I know Giselle is with me and together we will be able to keep each other safe, should the rumours of this place be true.

'Do you think the Hell Fire Club is real?' I ask Giselle, as I take my first few steps inside.

'I am real,' she replies, 'so doesn't that mean the Hell Fire Club might be real too?'

We both pause and think about that for a moment.

'All the bad people in my life are visible,' I whisper, 'so if there is something in there that's invisible, then I am not too worried about it. I do live with the Enemy after all, so this can't be worse than that, right?'

As we make our way further inside, there is an eerie silence intermittently punctuated by the rustling sound of Ruth digging deep into her almost-finished packet of crisps. Ruth always has a way of making her snacks last longer than anybody else. I enjoy eating mine fast, and when my cheeks are nice and full, the distractions from the outside world are drowned by the sound of my crunching and chewing, and for a moment I am in a sort of peace.

We make it across the hall and into a large reception room where a giant fireplace stands tall. There is light coming in from a tiny stone window to our right, and the light behind me causes my shadow to appear on the large stones under our feet. There are two massive stones holding up an even larger single stone, and this is the centrepiece of this allegedly haunted building, and of all the Hell Fire Club tales.

This house was built in 1725 by William Connolly and during its construction the builders decided to use stones from a nearby cairn and a prehistoric passage grave. But shortly after completion, a storm blew the roof off the house and local superstition attributed this to the work of the devil as a punishment for interfering with the cairn.

The house was left for the next ten years, for fear of angering the devil further. Then a group calling themselves the Hell Fire Club took possession of the building. They had no issue with the devil and during their gatherings they always left a seat empty at their table, should the devil ever show up. The building burnt down a few years later, and though there are many stories as to how the fire started, nothing has ever been proven. The house was abandoned again, and this time left to fall into ruin. And here I am now, around 280 years later, standing in front of the fireplace that may be connected to the devil.

'Are you all right, Flynner?' I hear Simon calling out to me. 'Have you seen the devil?'

'No,' I answer back. 'Well, not yet anyway.'

'Don't go too far, don't get yourself lost in there', cautions Ruth, concerned she would be the one who would have to explain to Mam or John where I was – or wasn't.

I can hear Ruth tell Simon that she doesn't want to retrieve me if I get in trouble, and that he will have to be the one to recue me should I need help.

'Who's that?' I ask Giselle as a figure moves in the shadows. I'm not afraid, even though I am standing in almost pitch darkness in one of Ireland's most haunted buildings. In my everyday life, I would often see shadows in shadows, faces in reflections and shapes in darkness, so this was a familiar experience.

'Hello?' I call out in the direction of the shadow, but there is no answer. I can see the shape standing still and facing me, but I can't hear anything.

'You try,' I say to Giselle.

'Hello,' she says, 'are you okay?'

Silence. But I can tell that Giselle is listening as if the shadow is talking back to her.

'I know,' she says eventually. 'It's okay, it's safe.' She then turns to me, and says, 'This is Abigail.'

As the shadowy shape moves out of the darkness and into the light, I begin to see her face, her black hair and blue eyes, her soft young pale skin, her almost perfect rounded cheekbones. Now that we've been introduced, I can hear her when she tells me she is the same age as Giselle and me. She tells us how she has been alone for a long time, waiting to belong, waiting to feel connected to something, but being invisible makes this so difficult.

She echoes the words of the lady from London, and it makes me think there is a world full of the invisible who are desperately hoping to be heard and seen. Some are, but for a limited time, and then they are forgotten and left to wander alone.

'We see you,' we reassure her. 'You can belong with us.'

By now my parents and Leah have made it up the hill and found Ruth and Simon outside the entrance, without me. I can hear the muffled sounds of shouting, the very sound I often listen to lying in my bed at night. When their voices sound far away, I feel safe, but when they become clearer, when I can hear the words they are screaming at each other, I no longer feel secure.

'Jonathan!' shouts John. 'What are you messing at in there?' He's angry, and I can hear him coming to get me.

He finds me standing by the fireplace talking to Abigail and Giselle, but all he sees is me, standing alone in an empty room talking to myself. Already annoyed from fighting with Mam all morning and frustrated at the inconvenience of having to find me, he grabs me by the shoulder and drags me out to where everyone else is waiting.

I can tell from their faces that in the short time between my parents arriving at the ruin and my father getting me out, the atmosphere has completely changed. Simon and Ruth look like they have been crying. Our excitement and wonder for this place that was so vivid only moments ago has now vanished. The place we were escaping from on this Sunday morning adventure has followed us here and drowned out our happiness, again.

'Is it always like this?' asks Abigail, once we get home.

'Always,' replies Giselle.

'In a minute John will look for a hug to make himself feel

better, just like he always does when he goes back to normal,' I say.

'One day you need to not let him forgive himself, let him feel a fraction of how we feel every day,' says Giselle.

'We do have another place we can go to, that's never sad,' I say to Abigail.

'Then why don't you just go and live there?' she asks.

I look at Giselle, and say to Abigail: 'I don't know, maybe we should?'

Living in Domdie all the time hadn't occurred to me until then, and it wouldn't be the last time I'd consider it.

CHAPTER 7

Pushed Through a Door

1986 (age six)

And so the months pass, with my parents' relationship deteriorating every day, or so it seemed to me. The only things keeping me going are Giselle, Abigail, my group of girlfriends at school, and my siblings. Also, I have a third invisible friend called Florence. Giselle and I met her on an island Simon and I visited on our last family holiday to Lough Key Forest Park. My brother and I would sneak out of our cabin in our pyjamas and oversized orange life jackets and climb down to our hire dinghy and row into the abyss of adventure, and this is where we found our island.

Beyond a perimeter of trees were the remains of a small castle. You couldn't see this from the water's edge, so the only way to know it was there was if you'd ventured in.

It was the first time we did this that I met Florence. We had just come across the ruins.

'Wow, do you think there is treasure here?' Simon asked.

'There has to be,' I said, excitedly. 'Maybe we're the first people to find this place.'

Simon began to climb up the wall to see what lay on the other side.

'Be careful, Simon, it doesn't look too safe,' I said to him, worried he might fall.

Simon was never afraid of anything, always the brave one, so he continued up. I kept watching until he climbed over the edge. Giselle appeared by my side just as Simon disappeared out of sight.

'Simon!' I shouted. 'Are you okay?' But all I got back was silence.

Standing there, on what now felt like a deserted island, the once peaceful sounds of nature began to sound threatening, especially as Giselle had begun to wander off. I could feel the grip of anxiety beginning to take hold of me, smothering my adventurous spirit. I started to panic and then I heard a voice.

'You're not on your own.'

It sounded like it came from inside the castle, so I took a step closer and looked deep within the shadows of the decaying walls.

'Giselle,' I said, speaking into the darkness, 'is that you?'

But this voice was different, not Giselle's whispered gentle tone; this was more assertive and direct.

'No, not Giselle,' the voice announced.

And then from out of the archway, a young girl appeared.

'Hello, Jonathan,' she said stepping closer to me.

Unlike how I usually feel when a new person breaks into my space, I was calm, almost at peace, and the closer she came to me, the warmer I felt. She made me feel the same way Giselle did when she was near me.

'My name is Florence,' she said, reaching out her hand. I reached back and we touched.

She has been coming to Domdie with Giselle and me ever since, and keeping me company at home too. She's wiser than us, and reassuring too. I feel lucky to have her in my life.

And then something dramatic happens to me, one of those life-defining moments. It is one of those sliding-door situations. I wonder who I would be today if I hadn't been pushed through that particular door.

It's a spring morning in my last year at Presentation. I am sitting on a grey plastic chair surrounded by twenty-five other boys, some of whom I know from my current school class. We are all packed into a giant school auditorium at Terenure

College, which also serves as a theatre, an indoor football space and an exam hall. On this occasion the enormous room is being used to host the 1986 entrance exams for potential future attendees of this private boys' school in south County Dublin. Presentation only allows the girls to progress into the junior school; the boys must leave. How do I explain I am not one of the boys? I wanted things to stay as they were, connected with my girl friends. They are what helps me cope with what's going on at home, and now I am being ripped out from that bubble and forced to assimilate here.

Everything about this school is terrifying to me. If you didn't feel intimidated passing though the imposing black iron gates at the school entrance, or the rows of aggressive rugby pitches or the ominous grandeur of the main building, then the height of the ceiling in this hall, where I now sit, will surely be the thing that unnerves you. I feel microscopic and helpless.

It's a surprisingly warm day and the sun is beaming into the hall through the large windows, and directly onto me. But this isn't bringing me joy. I feel like someone is holding a giant magnifying glass over me and intensifying my anxiety. The oversized clock above the stage is making an obtrusive ticking sound, and with each tick and tock I am kept conscious and stuck in this reality.

There is a pattern and flow to the clouds offering me a moment of respite from the sun's rays. I am hoping for some familiar rain, as the sound it makes on a windowpane always relaxes me and distracts my mind – the gentle pitter-patter helps me forget where I am. *Please let it rain!* Irish weather has the unique ability to achieve all four seasons in one day, so I am hopeful. But right now, the clouds won't cry for me. They let the sun continue its relentless assault.

On my desk is a pencil, a pen and a half-chewed hand-me-down eraser that had been my brother's. The boys beside me have posh little pots of Tipp-Ex. This is one of the many differences between me and the other boys sitting this exam. Another is that their school bags have distinctive football-related badges and stickers.

I always avoid answering: 'What club do you support?' Sometimes I just say a popular team name I had heard of. 'Manchester,' for example. But that comes with the risk that further questions might follow, like: 'United or City?' Why they couldn't just have one team per city, I never understood. What I do understand, better than any boy, is fancy paper collections.

I look over at Patrick who is sitting at the desk next to me. He is busy writing away with his fountain pen. I have a ballpoint pen because Mam doesn't trust me with changing the ink cartridge without getting ink on my hands, and then inevitably transferring it to my clothes, so she gave me a pen that doesn't require any skills other than holding it. Patrick's older brother is already attending the school, and because of Patrick's extremely positive reports from Presentation, this exam is just a formality as he has already been offered a place. But for me, with my not-so-positive reports and my attendance in the 'slow class', as I've heard people call it, I don't have an offer yet, even though my brother is already attending.

If I pass this exam, my parents will be happy, but in doing so I will cement a future for myself that will lead to me losing all of my friends and having to pretend to be someone I am not for the next twelve years. I'm not sure who thought it was a good idea to send someone like me to a boys' school like Terenure College, but my parents have a plan for me, my path is already programmed into the Satnav of Life and I am to just follow the route with the least resistance. Even though it is directing me to the correct destination, I think the route calculations might be off and I am being sent into gridlock.

As ever, the anxiety makes my mind wander, and I reach down into my satchel, in which I have a few loose daisies. Giselle appears, and I hand her the assortment I have collected for the daisy chains she makes. Florence says braiding is the best way to make a strong chain and this technique requires long thin stems, while Giselle always disputes this and says slitting makes a better chain, but this relies on a thicker stem. I don't really have a preference, as long as what I end up with is pretty, which isn't often, so I leave it up to Giselle and Florence. I do think we should add some other flowers between the daisies to mix it up a bit sometimes.

Giselle tells me I should fail the exam on purpose, and then I might be able to stay at Presentation with my friends, even though I am a boy, but Florence thinks that might make things worse, so I am not sure what to do.

I try to focus on what's written in the exam paper. I never really trust written words, especially on exams, because so often they trick me into writing the wrong things, and when I go back to check, they change into other words. But I have developed a strategy that sometimes works and gets me past my teachers. I focus on a few words per line and then just fill in the blanks with my mind, and if I am quick enough, I can do this before the words have time to change again. The downside is that once I write out my answer, those words can also change when I read them back. But right now, my method isn't working. I'm holding my pen, staring at the page blankly. Thirty minutes have already passed and all I have achieved is to write my name on the page, and I'm not even sure I have spelt that correctly.

Standing at the front of the hall is Father Kilmurray, the head teacher, surveying his future flock. He is dressed in an oversized brown tunic with a hood draped over his shoulders, and he wears a beaded cross around his neck. Terenure College is part of the Carmelite Order, so most of the teachers in the school are clergy. I watch as the boys who have already finished their exams walk up and hand him their papers enthusiastically. He looks pleased and pats them on their shoulders. There is a sense of familiarity between him and these boys, more than likely they have older brothers already attending, or maybe their families are the right kind of people for Terenure, and he can sense that.

After a while, there is just a handful of boys left and I still haven't decided what I should do, nor have I given any of the questions any thought. All I keep thinking is that I really don't want to be here or lose my friends. Perhaps Giselle is right and my only option is to fail the exam and wait for the consequences with my parents and hope that Presentation can make an exception for me, even though I am a boy. So, with my blue pen in my right hand, I begin my self-sabotage.

A few days have passed since the exam and I've heard nothing. I decide to forget all about it, but when I see the letter arrive, I panic. It is addressed to Master Joly - another reason why I shouldn't be attending this school. Being addressed as 'Master' might be an exciting moment for a different kind of boy, but for me it was depressing.

I knew I had to wait for my parents before opening it, but I had to know what was inside. Simon, who is mischievous, once showed me how to hold a letter over the kettle so the steam releases the adhesive, which means you can open the letter without tearing the envelope and then seal it up again as if nothing happened. So this is what I do. As I pull the letter out, time seems to slow and, for once, each word exposes itself to me in an ordered format. The school logo is prominent at the top centre of the page: an arm reaching out from a crown holding a blazing sword, with the school motto underneath: *Zelo Zelatus Sum Pro Domino Deo Exercituum* (which I now know is Latin for 'I Am Filled With Zeal For God, The King Of All Hosts')

March 16th, 1986

Dear Mr & Mrs Joly,

The admissions committee of Terenure College has reviewed your application and results of Master Joly's entrance exam. Unfortunately, at this time we will be unable to offer a placement for the coming school year.

I take my time to read the words over and over to be extra sure there is no chance that what I am reading could change. This is well and truly a letter of rejection; my self-sabotage was a success.

Filled with hope and a sense of excitement for the future, I close the letter up again, place it back, just inside the front door, and leave to tell my friends the good news. I know when my parents get home later there will be a price to pay, but I am willing to endure this if it means I can attend the right school. I made my own decision about my future and it feels strange. Maybe there is more I can do? Perhaps this is just the beginning?

A week has passed since I opened the letter, and yet nothing has been said to me. I have been waiting for the Enemy to strike, but instead an eerie peace has descended on the house. One afternoon after school, Mam says we are going somewhere, and it sounds serious. I've been told to get dressed into a shirt and a pair of trousers and to brush my hair. I really want to wear the unicorn shoes I borrowed from my friend Sophie because my shoes are always plain and boring. When my parents found them, I had to pretend I didn't know where they came from. They ended up in Ruth's wardrobe, but right now I know better than to put them on, despite Giselle urging me to do the opposite.

We're taking the car, so we must be going a fair distance. For some reason I don't ask her where we're going. I've got the window open, and I am leaning slightly out, as usual. My head is pointed upwards towards the sky, so the wind is brushing over me and drowning out the sound of the world, just as I like it. This is the same sensation I get when I stand under a shower and position myself so both ears are covered by the flowing water and it feels like I am blasting off, leaving this world behind.

As usual, Mam drives like she's in a racing car. She is particularly dramatic in the shifting of gears, as if she were in an international competition. I know when the race is about to begin when she slams her left foot into the floor, followed by the climactic thrashing of the gear stick into position. Sometimes the car lets out a crunching cry when she misses, and back in goes the foot and the process repeats itself.

As we reach the top of Fortfield Road, the car starts to slow and the wind that was soothing me begins to die down, and the noise of the world increases. Mam turns into a side road and now I am starting to think I've got this all wrong, we must be collecting Simon as we are turning into the drive of Terenure College.

Mam parks the car and gets out, indicating for me to follow. There is a silence to the school that doesn't feel natural.

Although there are around a thousand boys in there right now, it almost feels like we are alone.

'Doesn't anyone have any fun here?' asks Giselle. It seems to be a reasonable question.

We walk into the main entrance and as I step inside, I look over to my right and I am reminded of the day I sat the entrance exam. The hall door is open and I can see into the room that almost became my undoing, but thankfully I was able to save myself that day, and while I will be sad not to attend the same school as my brother, this is for the best. In front of me is a spiral staircase made out of marble, and to the left is a dark corridor. I look in both directions wondering where Simon will appear from.

We are approached by a teacher, dressed in the same oversized brown tunic as Father Kilmurray had been wearing. He asks us to follow him, and he takes us into the dark corridor. We walk through several more poorly-lit corridors, go up stairs and down stairs, and eventually stop in front of a large door. There are no windows or lights leading up to this door, so it is completely dark. As it opens, the light from inside the room almost blinds me for a moment; all I can see is the figure of a giant man standing in front of me. As my eyes adjust, I realise this is Father Kilmurray. I think to myself, *Simon must have done something really bad.*

I am offered a seat. Mam sits down in the chair next to me, and the adults begin talking. I am asked what I like about school and what my favourite subjects are. Do I enjoy sports, and have I ever played rugby? I try not to laugh while Giselle acts out, pretending to speak when he speaks, and this is making me feel relaxed. Usually I would feel cautious and nervous to talk so freely to someone like Father Kilmurray, but because I have failed the exam, I know this is just small talk while we wait for Simon to join us. I speak about my friends and the subjects I like, and how I have always done well at school sports days, and then he says something, and I realise what this is. He's obviously figured out I didn't fail my entrance exam because I didn't know the answers, I failed it on purpose. With my guard down, I have been my most confident, and without realising it in time, I have undone my self-sabotage and am on the verge of securing a place. Mam smiles as I do her proud, winning the room, undoing the mistake.

And then Father Kilmurray asks me this:

'And if you were to join your classmates this year, would you be willing to give it your best effort?'

There is still a chance I can dismantle this disaster and avoid becoming Master Joly, but looking over at my mam, so happy, so proud of me, I can't bring myself to disappoint her. So I reply with a positive 'Yes, Sir!'

And that was that. I was in. My heart sank.

I know now that there was never going to be another option than to attend this school. Mam must have worked hard to get this interview and straighten out my destiny. But I can't help but wonder what would have happened had I ended up in some other mixed-sex school and continued to have friends I could relate to.

Regardless, the positive outcome that ultimately came out of this particular door opening was that it pushed me further into Domdie, and with that, closer to the people who ended up saving my life.

CHAPTER 8

The Unhappy Law

1986 (age six)

Since I accidentally became Master Joly, I'm finding my final weeks at Presentation hard, knowing my time with my friends has a fixed expiry date. Most of the girls are preparing for their future school life together, breaking into two groups: one for the girls that are staying here in Presentation and one for the girls who are moving on to Our Lady's. But there is no group for me.

We are sitting at the back of St Joseph's Church doing a rehearsal for next month's communion service, at which I will have my first holy communion. I live in a village that has three churches, but only one shop. I was baptised in St Pius', that's the church John usually drags us to whenever he wants to make us look like good Catholics. But in truth, religion doesn't have a place in our home. I find that what the priest says about living our lives 'soothingly and reassuringly', or with kindness and happiness, or how above all we must be good people, doesn't make much sense because my world is filled with unhappiness, and the only good people I know are invisible. And one of them is here with me now.

'Maybe you should try to talk to the boys,' Abigail says, who I have come to learn is more practical than Florence and Giselle. 'Make a better effort to be part of that group.'

'They just make fun of me all the time,' I say, demoralised.

I look over at a group of boys sitting together at the back of the church, exchanging football stickers and not listening to the instructions being given by our teacher. I'm trying to imagine myself assimilating into their world, being a boy.

'Isn't that the same as your fancy paper collection?' Abigail is trying to help me make a connection in the real world. 'Maybe you might like football?'

'But I don't know how to be a boy,' I say.

'You could always pretend? Make it a game.'

'Games are meant to be fun,' Giselle chimes in, obviously not too happy with the idea of pretending to enjoy something, and because playing that game would require silence from her.

I can already feel a distance growing between me and my

girl friends, with their excited chatter about what going to secondary school will be like. I feel so left behind, and I've not even left yet.

'Do *you* know what it is?' Emma is speaking to me, but I haven't been paying close enough attention to their conversation.

Grace answers instead. 'My mam told me it's when a mam and a dad don't get along anymore, so they go to live in different houses.'

'What are you talking about?' I ask.

'Divorce,' answers Grace, with a confidence and excitement that comes from knowing something the rest of us don't.

'I think my parents should do this,' I say back to her, thinking about what life would be like if my parents didn't live together.

'I don't think you're allowed,' says Gemma, who is sitting on the other side to me. 'I heard my mam and dad talking about voting for it, or something,' she continues.

'You have to vote to live in different houses?' I ask, slightly confused. 'Shouldn't people just . . . be happy where they want?'

'I think it's against the law,' says Grace.

'It's against the law to be happy?' I say. 'That's stupid.' I know if my parents were to get a divorce and live in different houses, there would be a lot more peace. If they stopped fighting with each other, then maybe they would also stop fighting with me.

A few days later Mam and I go to Penneys, the department store, for an outfit for the holy communion. The invisible friends are excited to see what we get, but I'm not so excited.

All my school friends will be wearing white dresses, like mini wedding dresses to marry God, but there is no chance I will get to dress like them.

'We would look amazing in one of those dresses!' says Giselle to me, as we admire the rows of white communion dresses hanging in a row and the small group of young girls with their mams, also shopping for this important milestone in their lives.

'I was planning to wear Ruth's socks but I don't think they will be enough to make me feel pretty like them,' I say sadly.

'Do you want to get a divorce if they vote for it?' I ask Mam as she pulls out different blazers from the boys' rack nearby.

She stops what she's doing and turns to look at me.

'Where did you hear that word?' she asks in a shocked tone.

'Grace told me that when mams and dads are unhappy together, they can get one and live in different places and be happy.'

She paused. 'Divorce will only be for the rich people, so it's not something we need to worry about,' she mutters as she hands me a grey shirt and a blazer then hurriedly adds, 'We don't have your Terenure uniform yet, so you can just wear this. There is no point in getting a whole new outfit if you can't wear it next year, it's a waste of money.'

Giselle rolls her eyes and sighs dramatically.

'Don't listen to her, Jonathan,' says Abigail. 'It might be better to just try to fit in, you're going to Terenure in Sep-tember either way.'

'Remember what the priest said about happiness . . . it's important,' says Giselle to her, gesturing over to where the girls' white dresses are hung.

'But that's what brings out the Enemy,' Abigail says, pointing at the clothes I am holding in my arms.

'Fuck the Enemy,' announces Giselle, and as she says it, I drop the clothes I am holding. I know this is a bad word, and I've never heard a child say it. I've certainly never heard Giselle use it before.

'What are you doing?' Mam calls back to me. 'Pick them up!' I look up at Mam, terrified.

'Tell her!' instructs Giselle, clearly on a roll.

I take a deep breath. 'I don't want to wear this,' I say sheepishly.

'Why not? You'll look handsome and all of your friends will be wearing the same thing,' she says as she picks the clothes back up, looking around to make sure no one she knows saw me acting up.

'They are *not* my friends, and I don't want to be handsome . . .' I pause and take a deep breath. 'I want to be pretty.' I can't believe I actually said it.

I can hear Giselle whooping next to me, but my mam glares.

'Don't be silly, you're not a girl, Jonathan,' says Mam.

I take another deep breath. 'How do you know?'

Mam is getting more uncomfortable because we're having this conversation in public. She leans in and says, 'I'm your mother, you came out of me, I think I would know if you were a girl,' laughing at the idea of her second son being a girl.

Humiliated and disappointed, I turn to Giselle. 'It's no use, no one will listen to us.'

'So just play along until you don't have to anymore,' suggests Abigail, ever practical. 'It might not be that bad.'

But while I am standing there in silence, something surprising happens. I've since realised that my mam must have taken a moment to review the conversation and thought about what I wanted, or at least what she thought I wanted.

'Follow me,' she says, as she walks around the shop from aisle to aisle, picking out items from various racks. I think

I'm in trouble, so I don't pay attention to what she chooses; anyway, I'm sure they're just more boring grey clothes for boys. We go to the changing room at the back of the shop and she hands me her selection of clothes. 'Try these on,' she says as she pulls the curtain open for me to walk inside.

I step into the small changing cubical and put the clothes on the black plastic chair, expecting the worst, but then I notice she has picked out a white jumper, white trousers, a white shirt and white runners. It's not the pretty white dress that my friends will be wearing, but it's also not the grey suit that the boys will be wearing either. it's something in the middle, which is how I feel most of the time – not a boy but also not a girl. I am something in the middle.

While I am in the changing room, I overhear Mam talking to another mother about the people who don't want the unhappy law, as I call it, to end.

'They are all gathered in the city centre,' says the other mother.

'Wouldn't be surprised if he was there too,' Mam says. 'This isn't something he will want for us, but I will be voting for it.'

I don't hear the rest of the conversation, because I'm too busy trying on the clothes, which all seem to fit me perfectly. We leave Penneys with the white outfit, and I am over the moon.

*

It's now the morning of my first holy communion and I am sitting in the church, waiting for the priest to call us forward and put the little disc of bread in our mouths. As we get called up, I can see all the other boys dressed in suits, some black, some grey and some in their uniforms for next year. Meanwhile, I am standing in all white next to my friends in their pretty white dresses. I almost blend into the girl group. Something about me feels different. It is like I am being myself for the first time, here in the real world.

'Why isn't there a group for people like me?' I ask Abigail. She always has good answers.

'Because nobody else wants an enemy like you have, and they know if they join your group they too will become a target, so they choose to hide,' she replies.

'So it's like another unhappy law then,' I say.

It is the day of the vote and John has brought the television from the sitting room into the kitchen so that he and Mam can watch the results come in live while Mam cooks. There is a man with big glasses sitting behind a desk talking directly to the camera. He introduces himself as Pat Kenny, and he is commenting live as the counting begins. I look at both of my parents to see if I can gauge their emotional state, wondering if I need to hide. Mam looks nervous but with an element of hope for the future, while John looks unimpressed, as if this is just a waste of time.

'Okay, so we have the first results in,' announces Pat Kenny. 'It's Dublin South, and the count is 23,248 "no" and 27,768 "yes", so that's a yes for Dublin South.'

'Is that us?' I ask my mother proudly.

'No, but it's very near us,' she whispers with a smile.

'It's a good start,' whispers Giselle.

'Let's hope it keeps going in the right direction,' I say to her.

'And we have another result in,' says Pat Kenny.

The atmosphere in the kitchen is getting tense now, and I know that if the results continue in this direction the Enemy will probably arise, but if it means I will go with Mam to her new house, it might be worth it.

'It's Dublin again,' he says, 'Dublin South East, and the result is 16,464 "no" and 19,107 "yes", so again that's another yes.'

'Is that us?' I ask again.

'No, not us, but close,' she replies. John looks at me as if to tell me to be quiet.

The next four more results came in from Dublin North, North East, South East and Dun Laoghaire, all with a winning 'yes' vote, so it is looking very likely that the unhappy law will be changed, and all the mams and dads who don't get along will no longer have to live together and get angry at their children.

I leave the kitchen and skip to my room to plan for what will be my future.

'This is exciting,' I say to Giselle, as we play with my soft toys.

'Do you think we will stay here with Mam or John, or do you think we will go to a new house with one of them?' she asks.

'Shouldn't we wait to find out if it's actually happening before we make plans?' cautions Abigail.

She's always more sensible than Giselle and me. But I don't want to be sensible.

'You heard the man on television, it's happening!' I say. I give Lambsy a big hug.

'I know, I just don't want you to get hurt,' she says.

'What are you going to wear to the new house?' asks Giselle. She clearly doesn't want to be sensible either.

'Jonathan!' calls Mam from the kitchen. 'They're about to announce our area.'

I go back to the kitchen, and stand by my mam, looking up at the television. John has lost interest and left the room, so it is just the two of us. There is a large board next to the table where Pat Kenny is sitting, and there is a woman who is marking down the results as they come in. So far, six results and six 'yes' votes. Even though I am still young, I know this is really important.

'Dublin South Central,' Pat says. 'And the count there is 21,945 "no" and 19,207 "yes", so we have our first "No" win for Dublin.'

We let that sink in for a bit.

'Was that us?' I ask Mam, confused.

'Yes,' she says, in a defeated tone.

John enters the kitchen again.

'What's happening?' he asks, with a newfound confidence. 'Have they come to their senses, finally?'

I stand there watching as each county, town and city is called, and with each announcement my heart sinks a little:

Carlow: NO, Cavan: NO, Cork: NO, Donegal: NO, Galway: NO, Kerry: NO, Kildare: NO, Laois: NO, Limerick: NO, Longford: NO, Louth: NO, Mayo: NO, Meath: NO, Roscommon: NO, Sligo: NO, Tipperary: NO, Waterford: NO Wexford: NO, Wicklow: NO.

There is a total of 1,482,644 votes cast, and of that 538,279 are for 'yes' and 935,843 are for 'no'. Therefore, the unhappy law will remain.

I look at my parents' faces to see their reaction. John looks relieved, while Mam looks disheartened.

'I guess Mam and John will be staying unhappy,' I say to Giselle.

'And us too,' she says gently.

CHAPTER 9

Sheep to the Wolves

1986 (age six)

I'm back in the hall of Terenure College where I failed my entrance exam a few months ago. It's the first day of the new term. I walked here this morning with Simon. He left me in the hall and went on up to his class. I am still confused as to what I am doing here. I look around at the boys trying to find their names on the class lists that are printed out and stuck to a wooden board at one end of the hall. I go to join them.

The classes are split into three groups: 2X, 2Y and 2Z. I read though the list and see I am joining 2Y. Also on the same list are Patrick, Seán, Peter and Stephen, all boys from my class in Presentation, but I've never really spoken to any of them.

'Maybe Abigail was right, maybe you should have made friends with those boys before you left Presentation,' whispers Florence, rather unhelpfully in my opinion.

I never did talk to them, because I had still thought there would be a way out. But as the summer came and went, and September rolled around driven forward by the unstoppable force that is time, my hope faded and now here I am.

'Do you see my group?' I ask Giselle.

'I can't see anything in here, there are too many people,' she replies, 'and everyone is dressed the same too.'

And then through the crowd I see Patrick waving at me. He must know I am in his group and, noticing that I am looking a bit lost, he signals to me. I haven't spent much time with him apart from the awkward moments when my mam would talk to his mam, pretending we are going to be best friends.

'Maybe he isn't that bad,' I say to Giselle.

'Yeah, maybe this won't be that bad,' she echoes.

I wave back, maybe a bit too enthusiastically, but I am excited that perhaps I was wrong all this time, perhaps this will be okay.

He looks back at me, confused, and lowers his hand slowly.

Still waving, I say to Giselle, 'He wasn't waving at me, was he?' just as Seán pushes past me and walks over to Patrick. They both look back at me.

'Stop waving,' says Giselle.

Father Kilmurray comes walking into the room and everyone stops their chatter and a silence falls on the great hall. I'm not sure if this is out of fear or respect. He walks past the groups of new boys, acknowledging the siblings of current students. He is followed by two senior students dressed in the school's rugby kit. They climb the five steps up onto the stage and pause a moment to take in the sea of fresh faces waiting for their leader to say something.

While everyone is standing to attention, I navigate my way over to the 2Y group and stand just outside the circle, wanting to stay out of focus.

'Oggy Oggy Oggy!' shout the two boys suddenly.

'Oi Oi Oi!' replies the hall, apart from me, in perfect synchrony.

'Oggy Oggy Oggy!' shout the boys again.

'Oi Oi Oi!' replies the room.

I have no idea what is happening. I feel like I am part of a ritual ceremony that everyone understands except me.

'What is going on?' I ask Giselle, completely confused. 'Are we supposed to know this?'

'Maybe just shout back "Oi Oi Oi" the next time?' she suggests helpfully.

I agree with her that that's a good idea. I turn back towards the stage, ready to join in.

'Oggy!' shout the boys on the stage.

'Oi!' replies the room, but while everyone else stops at just one 'Oi', I continue twice more. Patrick looks over at me and rolls his eyes. How did everyone know to stop at one?

'Oggy!'

'Oi!' This time I get it right.

'Is this all we do all day in this school?' asks Giselle.

'Oggy Oggy Oggy!'

'Oi Oi Oi!'

Father Kilmurray steps forward as the hall settles back into silence again.

'Welcome, young masters, to Terenure College,' he announces, and the hall erupts into a cheer. His voice has a softness to it, but his eyes say otherwise. I've seen that same look many times before in my father's eyes.

'This is the beginning of an exciting chapter in your lives. Here you will go from being boys to men and hopefully win a few rugby trophies along the way.'

'Wouldn't it be better if they just let people decide what they want to be?' I say to Giselle, referring to the fact that neither of us wants to be a part of this exciting chapter in our lives in which we become men.

'It would probably help if we were an actual boy in the first place,' she says.

'TE-RE-NU-RE!' the senior boys now shout out.

'TE-RE-NU-RE!' the freshers shout back.

It feels like we are an army preparing for battle, and I am the lost soldier who ends up here by mistake because my mam filled in the wrong form. I don't want to go to battle, I just want to be back with Grace, Gemma and the others and talk about fancy paper and play with our dolls. Instead I am here, standing to attention and awaiting my orders.

Father Kilmurray continues to talk about the school and their rugby ambitions. The two boys who did the shouting step forward again.

'We expect everyone to do at least a trial,' one of them says before the other one starts barking again:

'Everywhere we go, people always ask us . . .'

'Who we are, and where do you come from,' everyone around me chants. I have no idea how they know what to say.

'And we always tell them . . .' the boy continues.

'We're from TERENURE!' cries out the hall. And then there is a lot of screaming, clapping and shouting.

I'm kind of scared now, like we're in a cult and there's no way out. I find myself wishing Simon had prepared me.

But it seems the tribal war cries are over. We are led out of the hall and up the giant marble stairs, the same stairs I looked up while waiting for Simon on the day I accidentally got myself enrolled in this school. At the top of the stairs, we take a left turn on to a corridor with eight rooms. Each room has a number and a gold metal letter attached to the door. A teacher shouts out which form goes in which classroom.

'There is a lot of shouting at this school,' I whisper to Giselle, thinking about my day so far and how I miss the calm and gentle approach to school life that Presentation accustomed me to.

Unlike Presentation, we are not assigned desk partners, because each table is for a single person. The cliques gather and choose desks close together, while I and a few others like me who don't look like they are supposed to be here stand at the door, waiting for someone to tell us where to go.

'For God's sake, take a bloody seat,' says the teacher as he comes into the room. 'This isn't baby school anymore, you need to man up if you want to be a Terenure boy, we don't have time to be girls here.'

I quickly look around to check he's not talking to me personally. I am slightly worried he knows I am a girl, and that this remark is directed at me.

'Maybe it would all work out if he knew,' whispers Giselle. 'Then they would have to move us back to our friends. Maybe you should tell him?'

'That's a bad idea,' says Abigail. 'Take that seat,' she says bossily as she points over to a desk near the front of the class.

There are windows on three of the four sides of the room that look like the best place to sit – I could stare outside and wait for time to pass by – but the desks there have already been taken. I sit myself down where Abigail told me to go.

The desk and chair are connected by a metal pipe, and the desktop opens upwards to reveal a storage compartment where you place your bag, but not your lunch because this school has its own canteen. The boys settle down.

'Good morning, gentlemen,' says the teacher as he sits on his desk with a cool demure, indicating he is the kind of man we should all look up to – a Terenure man. 'My name is Mr O'Leary, and I will be your form teacher for this year. I like to start off each year by getting everyone to introduce themselves.'

He pulls out a class list from his leather satchel.

'So, one at a time, when I've called your name, I want you to stand up, say your name, and tell me what your father does for a living. Let's start with Alan Murphy.'

The boy called Alan Murphy stands up. He seems confident and eager to please.

'Hello, my name is Alan, and my dad is a doctor.'

Mr O'Leary looks at him approvingly.

'Good stuff, Alan,' says Mr O'Leary, 'maybe you will follow in his footsteps one day.'

Alan sits back down with a smile on his face.

'Okay, next up is Eamon O'Shea,' announces Mr O'Leary.

The boy called Eamon jumps up – another one who looks very self-assured.

'Hi, my name is Eamon, and my dad is an accountant.'

It continues this way for a while, and I see a pattern emerging: these boys are very sure of themselves and surrounded by their own kind. Except for me, I am not part of this, I am the imposter. The only reason my parents can afford to send me here is because both my parents have jobs, not just my dad. But no one is asking what our mams do for a living, because I don't think any of them apart from mine works.

Suddenly, it's my turn.

'Jonathan Joly,' announces Mr O'Leary.

'Lie,' says Giselle.

'Don't,' says Abigail.

I try to ignore their voices.

'That's me, Sir,' I say as I stand up.

'No one will know,' continues Giselle.

'Hi, my name is Jonathan, and my dad works . . . in television,' I say.

'Interesting,' replies Mr O'Leary as he leans forward. I have got his full attention.

'You see, I told you,' says Giselle. I wish she would be quiet as I am finding it quite hard to concentrate on what's going on. I am unnerved by Mr O'Leary's interest.

'In what capacity?' asks the teacher. 'Do we have a famous person's son in the class?'

'He installs them!' someone behind me calls out. 'He drives a van, Sir.'

There is a burst of chuckling from the class, as if the fact that someone's dad drives a van is something to be laughed at.

I turn to see who called me out, and I see that it was the boys from Presentation, Patrick and Seán. They know my family, know what I am like and because I am different to them, that means I am a target. Suddenly a large spotlight is shining on me, and I can feel the anxiety searing throughout my body. Everyone is looking at me, waiting to see what is going to happen.

'This isn't good,' says Giselle.

Mr O'Leary has decided to ignore what Patrick and Seán have said.

'Well?' he perseveres. 'What is it? What does he do in television?'

'He makes televisions work,' I answer, but I'm aware I say

this as a question rather than a statement, betraying my lack of confidence.

'Right, so he doesn't work on television or even in television,' says the teacher.

'No, Sir,' I reply.

Mr O'Leary stares hard at me. I await my fate. What he says next makes my anxiety levels soar.

'Right, come up here.'

I struggle to climb out of my table and chair unit, which fuels more laughter from the class. In terms of making first impressions, I know instinctively that this is going to be a hard one to overcome.

'This feels like an Enemy situation,' says Giselle, as I drag myself to the front of the class. She walks with me as she says, 'I thought enemies were only at home.'

I reach Mr O'Leary's desk after what feels like the long walk of shame. He stands up and towers over me.

'It was Jonathan, right?' he asks.

'Yes, Jonathan, Sir,' I reply. I can feel my palms getting sweaty. Mr O'Leary turns to face the classroom.

'One thing we don't want here in Terenure is liars, so let me demonstrate with Jonathan the consequences of telling lies.'

He turns to me again.

'Hold out your right hand, young man,' he orders.

I nervously do what he says, unsure of what is about to happen.

'May I borrow this?' the teacher asks to one of the boys sitting at the front as he picks up his wooden ruler. Without waiting for an answer, he comes back towards me.

'Let this be a lesson to you all,' he declares, raising the ruler high above his head and swiping it down swiftly so that it lashes on my knuckles with a loud smack.

As the ruler impacts with my skin, for a moment I am transported away from the classroom, away from the humiliation, and I am standing in an open field next to a large forest. The pain that suddenly overwhelms me is replaced by the soothing caress of Giselle's soft skin as she takes hold of my hand. I look around and surrounding me are all my invisible friends, together, giving me their strength.

And then with a blink of an eye I am back in the classroom, my injured hand still stretched out. I can see that it is red and throbbing, but I can't feel the pain. My invisible friends have taken the pain away for me. I look at the class and I realise that although I never expected to fit in here with the other boys – what I didn't expect was that the teachers would be enemies too.

'I have enemies at home, I have enemies at school,' I say to Giselle.

'There are no enemies in Domdie,' she whispers back.

Mr O'Leary interrupts our conversation.

'Now, don't cry like a girl,' he says, but I am not crying, and he is clearly confused as to why I am not making a sound, but I know he said this to get more laughs from the other boys in the classroom. He is enjoying the camaraderie among the boys as they watch me being punished.

'Right, boys,' he continues. 'Let's give Jonathan a clap for being a good example for us all.'

The classroom erupts in clapping and banging on the desks as I make my way back to my desk and I climb back into my cage, trying not to look at anyone.

'Now, who's next?' Mr O'Leary calls out. 'Ah yes, Patrick Doyle.'

Patrick stands up enthusiastically.

'My name is Patrick, and my dad is an architect.'

As I sit in my chair, I slowly start to slip away from the classroom and I am transported to Domdie, the place where I won't be ridiculed because of choices my parents made for their lives, that somehow reflects judgement onto me. The sound of Mr O'Leary's voice is being drowned out by the sound of the river I am sitting beside with my friends.

'Wasn't the best first impression,' I say to them.

'That was just the first day, it might get better,' says Abigail, always hopeful.

Giselle puts her hand on mine to try to cheer me up. 'How long do we have to come here for anyway?' she asks.

'I am in second class now.' I start to count, 'Four years of primary school, and then six years after that. So that's . . .'

'Ten years,' replies Florence, impatiently.

'Ten years!' I repeat, feeling overcome. I hadn't really thought about it to this extent, it's more years than I've already been alive. 'They can't make me do this.' I'm in despair.

'Let's take it day by day, there has to be some good here,' Florence soothes. 'Maybe you just need to try to fit in.'

'Yes, pretend to be like them,' echoes Abigail.

'Didn't pretending just get me smacked with a ruler?' I say, looking at my hand, and imagining this happening daily.

Giselle, sensing my spiral into the darkness, pulls me closer, turns to Abigail and Florence and says, 'If we all work together, we can survive.'

And just like that, things don't feel so unbearable anymore.

CHAPTER 10

John is Dead

1986 (age six)

'Anything yet?' I ask, looking over from behind our grey and black ten-inch plastic television.

Ruth and Simon are sitting on our old torn brown sofa, watching the static screen. It's quite early in the morning and the house is silent, apart from our excited chatter in the sitting room. Though it's only the 21st of December, the Christmas anticipation has injected us with an energy we can't control on this pre-dawn Sunday morning, which is why we are all awake. For me, this is the first time I've felt any joy or hope in what has been a first term of gloom.

We are each wearing our one-piece sleep suits which conveniently include feet coverings, so we are warm despite the lack of heating. The lights are still off and the only illumination is from the snowstorm patterns beaming from the television.

Now that Ruth is getting older, our parents thought it was time to separate the girls from the boys, so they have moved Simon and me into a bedroom on the ground floor, and Leah in with Ruth. I asked Giselle if she minded having to sleep with me in the boys' room, but she said it was okay, and that if we made a fuss about wanting to be in the girls' room the Enemy might surface, so it was best to pretend that we belonged in the boys' room.

Besides, Simon is nice, although he behaves like the bedroom is his. For example, there is a sink in it, but only Simon is allowed to use it. But I don't mind. To the left of the sink, there is a fireplace. No one ever uses it, except on Christmas Eve when Simon and I hold a plastic shopping bag with notes for Santa inside and let the chimney suck them up and send them off to the North Pole. It's worth being in the room just for that.

'Keep going,' says Simon. 'I think you're close.'

We are trying to change the channel to something we want to watch, and the only way to do that is to twist the little black plastic knobs that stick out of the back of the receiver. I am leaning over the small table that is holding the television in place. It's completely dark so I can't see the screen as I fiddle with the knobs, but I know to just keep twisting until someone tells me to stop.

'My fingers are killing me,' I whine.

'You have the smallest fingers, so you're best at this,' encourages Ruth, as if she were my own personal cheerleader.

'Wait, go back!' shouts Simon. 'I think I saw something.'

I don't understand why no one has invented a better way to change the channel. Maybe if people didn't watch as many videos, then they would figure out a better way, but I can't see that ever changing, and videos are so much more handy because you can put them on whenever you like, and when you need to use the toilet, you can pause the film. The number of TV shows and films I've partly missed over the years because of needing a wee or being late for the start is something that has always frustrated me.

'When I grow up, I am going to collect all the videos of all the shows and films I've missed and watch them all,' I mutter to Giselle while twisting the knobs.

Even though there are only three channels available, the treasure hunt feels endless due to the distance between channel frequencies.

Suddenly we hear the sound of a show ring though the static.

'Stop!' yells Simon. 'Go back a tiny bit.'

I take a deep breath and stretch my fingers out for one final twist. We don't know what channel we have stumbled upon, this could be *RTÉ News*, maybe even a church service, but then again it might be *Dempsey's Den*, or *The Muppet Babies* or even *SuperTed*. The longer the list of possible options gets the more excited I become, as I twist back and forth like a thief trying to crack a into a safe to retrieve not jewels or cash, but kids' TV.

Ruth is holding the *RTÉ* guide in her hand; the single most important publication in the entire country. This is the only directory of what's on and when, and is one of the most important structural components for entertainment at Christmas.

At the beginning of each December, we three sit together and take turns circling the shows we want to watch, starting from the beginning of the month right up to New Year's Eve. There are a few staples we always agree on, like the *Late Late Toy Show*. This is a must for us all. It's a three-hour live broadcast where the presenter invites children onto the show to test out all the new toys for Christmas. Knowing we are never going to get any of these toys, this makes for an enjoyable fantasy where we live vicariously through the lucky children.

These are our top ten picks from the *RTÉ Guide* this year:

TV Shows

Fraggle Rock

The Smurfs

Inspector Gadget

Trap Door

Punky Brewster

Movies

Indiana Jones and the Temple of Doom

Ghostbusters

NeverEnding Story

Herbie Goes Bananas

The Muppets Take Manhattan

But today, we're not fussed, any kids' programme will do. The screen comes to life as the channel lands its frequency. We can't quite tell what it is, but we know that it's not the news or a church service, so we are happy. Ruth is first to recognise the show, and in an excited gleeful yelp she shouts out:

'FAME! I want to live forever!'

Tuns out Simon is fussed when he realises what it is.

'Try again,' Simon says to me, directing me back to the television.

'No, I want to watch this,' protests Ruth, who has got up to dance like Coco.

As Simon and Ruth argue in the semi-darkness, I find myself drawn into the show. I like how the characters are dressed; even the boys are dressed in a cool way. Some of them even have long hair.

'Maybe I could be a dancer someday,' I say to Giselle, admiring their outfits.

Suddenly Mam comes in the door, crying and yelling.

'Dad's dead, he's gone, he's dead!'

She puts her arms around Ruth and Simon, scooping them up to their feet and looks over at me, indicating that I should join their circle of support. I stay where I am. I am not sure how to process this news, I don't know anyone who doesn't have a dad, so what will life be like now? I suppose there won't be an Enemy in the house, which is good news, but at the same time it also means nice John is also going to be gone and I like him.

Mam continues to sob. Ruth is the first to speak.

'What happened?'

'His heart gave out,' Mam answers hysterically. 'And he was driving, so he crashed his car.'

'How does your heart give out?' I ask Giselle.

She answers, 'That means it stopped.'

'Can it just stop, for no reason?'

I am starting to panic a little, wondering what if my own heart just stopped. I walk out from behind the television and over to the circle and join in, placing my arms around my siblings.

I can't stop asking Giselle the questions that are running through my brain as I scramble for meaning and reassurance.

'Doesn't your heart have something to do with love or being loved?

'What if I didn't feel love or even know what love was, does that mean my heart could just stop?

'Did my dad's heart stop because he didn't love me?

'But then again maybe if my heart stopped, I wouldn't feel sad any more, so maybe it's a good thing?'

Then the phone in the kitchen starts ringing and Mam releases us.

She stands and looks down at us through her tear-filled eyes. We are still embracing each other as we await her guidance.

'We will be okay,' she says. 'We will get through this,' she says.

And then she walks out of the door.

We are in stunned silence, not sure what to say or do. The sound of the television, which was drowned out by Mam's upset, comes back into focus now and draws our attention back to it.

Ruth, as always, steps up to look after us.

'Don't worry, guys, it will be okay,' she says, echoing our mother's words.

We sit back down on the sofa, in shock. The squabble about *Fame*, the excitement of tuning into a television channel, the magic of those days leading up to Christmas – all that is now forgotten and replaced with sadness and confusion.

All at once, the entire room is filled with a bright white light. I figure I am being transported to Domdie to help me escape this moment, but then I see that both Simon and Ruth are also reacting to the light. Maybe due to the gravity of the situation they also need Domdie in this moment, and somehow have been given the means to access it? I feel a brief sense of relief about sharing my world with them so I don't have to keep it a secret.

But then I realise that the light is coming from outside. A car has pulled into the driveway, and because we don't have curtains over our windows the room is filled with powerful glow of the headlights.

'Who's that?' asks Ruth.

'Probably Gramps,' replies Simon.

Our grandparents on John's side live across the street from

us and regularly look after us, so it makes sense that this might be them. In fact, they've probably spent more time with us than our actual parents now that Mam has gone back to work. The best thing about my grandparents is that when I knock on their door on the way back from somewhere, they give me 'a biscuit to cross the road'. I am not sure when this ritual started, but for as long as I remember I would stop off at theirs, be greeted warmly and then offered a chocolate chip cookie for the journey home, even though they lived less than a minute away from my house. I've often wondered how my father turned out the way he is, given how gentle and kind they are.

'But if it's Grandpa, why is he driving?' I ask out loud.

I wait for someone to explain, but no one does.

We take turns climbing up onto the window ledge to see who emerges from the car. But now that the car lights are turned off, we can't really tell. We hear the car door close with a loud slam, and then the sound of footsteps on the gravel driveway, but still can't see who the mysterious stranger is. We hear the front door open.

Whoever this is, they have a key to our house.

We rush nervously over to the sitting room door. The sitting room is right beside the main entrance, so we put our ears to the door to try to work out who is on the other side.

'Do you hear anything?' whispers Simon.

'Nothing,' replies Ruth.

I close my eyes and use my skills of detection. They have been sharpened through years of listening out for creaking floorboards and stairs, warning me that the Enemy might be invading imminently. Although our house has this carpet throughout, the floorboards under the carpet are loose in places and groan when walked on. Because of that I know every step in the house, and I can pinpoint anyone's location based on the sounds. It is like my own radar system for survival.

'Someone is coming,' I say.

We back away from the door and wait in suspense as the handle turns and the door opens slowly. I reach for Giselle's hand, the anticipation sending a familiar anxious spike, causing my heart to beat faster, my hand to begin sweating . . .

And then as the door opens fully, a large dark shadow is exposed, standing tall, holding a plastic bag in their right hand and the car keys in their left. We stand frozen in fear, no one makes a sound as we wait for something to happen.

The shadow moves into the room.

'What are you all doing up so early?' it demands.

'*AaaAAAahhhhAHHHHHAAaaaaaa!*' we scream. Standing in front of us is our father.

'What are you doing? Be quiet,' he says, getting annoyed with our misbehaviour.

'Mam said you were dead!' yelps Simon.

'What are you talking about?' asks John. 'Do I look dead?'

None of us has ever seen a dead person before, so how are we supposed to know? I have seen faces in the shadows, but this feels different; John is clearly here.

All the shouting catches the attention of my mam, and she comes back into the room.

'Dad's dead,' she says to him, crying.

'Oh Jaysus, no . . . What happened,' he asks.

'Happened this morning, the Gardai found him in his car, heart attack,' she sobs. 'Mam called me after they called her.'

'Ah sorry, love,' he says, as he put his arms around her in a rare moment of affection.

'I don't think it was our dad that died,' whispers Ruth.

'I think it's Dado,' says Simon.

Dado is our grandfather on my mam's side. We always called him Dado as he was an Irish preacher who was dedicated to giving his Catholic sermons in Gaeilge. Gaeilge is the original language spoken in Ireland. He was a good father to my mother, she always had him there as her ally even when Mamo would single her out and tell her she wasn't loved.

Just as Giselle and Domdie are here for me now. So, losing him will leave her alone with her husband, and no protector.

'Don't ever leave me,' I whisper to Giselle. 'Let's make a promise we will always be in each other's lives.'

I reach out and take Giselle's hand.

'I wouldn't be able to survive the Enemy, if your heart stopped.'

To this day, I do not understand why my mam led us to believe that it was my father who had died. Was it unconscious? Was that secretly what she was hoping for? Looking back, it makes me realise that our family was really quite dysfunctional in so many ways. But I also know that in all the confusion, I felt sorrow when I thought it was my father who had had an accident. And what that incident taught me was that there was still love in me for him.

CHAPTER 11

A Castle on an Island

1987 (age seven)

The last few months have been really testing at home. Any compassion John had for Mam after her father's death is long gone. They argue all the time now. Some days it even spills out into the driveway. I feel like everyone on our road knows our dark secret.

And despite Giselle's resolve to help us survive school by sticking together, it's still a miserable place for me. It is filled with bullies that hit and humiliate me daily, just for being me. And then at home there is no salvation or respite as I walk on eggshells, anxious I will be picked on.

Giselle has found a way to protect me a little bit: every so often, when I need a break, I let her take control of what we call my 'skin machine'. We discovered we could do this by accident after a particularly difficult morning at school. I spent a few hours in Domdie, while she took over my body and became me while I played with Florence and the others. To know this is something that can happen gives me huge relief.

Especially given what is happening this morning. Giselle and I are about to try on some of Ruth's clothes when I hear John come in the front door, and in my anxiety I knock over Ruth's doll's house. It makes a loud crash. John comes up to see what has happened and when he sees the doll's house in pieces on the floor he loses his temper and orders me to come downstairs to explain myself. Like every time, he is furious. His teeth are clenched, and his tongue is curled inside his bottom lip, pushing out his chin and lifting his cheeks. This is my forewarning that things are about to get bad.

The ground seems to shake underneath me as he stomps down the hallway.

'We could run to Domdie,' whispers Florence, looking at me, as I quickly put things away. It's tempting, but this time I know I shouldn't try to escape.

'I don't think that will end any better,' I reply shakily. 'No matter what I do or where I go, I always end up alone, with him.'

'You are not in this alone,' she says. 'We can help you – you are not trapped here. You can be free inside Domdie.'

I look away from Florence and make my way towards the stairs. I stop and sit down halfway, which is where I prefer to be when I'm about to get told off. I look at the wall beside me at the shadow I'm casting from the light from behind me. I wonder what kind of life the shadow me must be living: does he feel like I feel? Is he free? I raise my left hand and place it on the wall, it's almost like we are holding hands, me trapped in this world and him free in some other. I am preparing for the impending impact of my father's fist. I notice that the once light-green paint on the wall under my hand has almost faded away in its entirety. In some places the plaster has even come through, probably due to the number of times I have used this wall to catch myself after losing balance. The advantage of sitting on the stairs is that I can't fall backwards, but I can fall sideways. Therefore the best option is to use the wall as a support.

Ready and braced, I turn back to Florence.

'I want that to be true,' I say. 'I want a way out of this world.'

Florence gently runs her fingers over my hand. The sensation of her touch and our connection can keep out most of the darkness that obscures my reality, but even with her warmth and protection, the Enemy breaks through. It's the one thing my invisible friends can't seem to do – shield me in the physical world.

Florence grips my hand tighter, letting me know she is still there, supporting me as best she can. John is at the bottom of the stairs, his face level with mine, and suddenly I feel him spitting on me.

'You're a fucking mistake, you should have never been born!' he shouts at me.

For the first time we have reached an understanding: I too believe there has been a mistake. Whoever chooses where to send the new babies, which families they are to be born into, clearly made an error. And not only that, I also might have been sent in the wrong body.

'Why can't you just do as you're fucking told?' he continues. 'Why do you always have to make every fucking little thing so difficult?'

I look over at Florence but she is helpless to protect me. I turn back to look for my shadow friend, but the light has faded and he is gone. I am on my own.

The Enemy puts his left hand on the banister, giving him leverage to lean in further.

'You are the fucking reason why your mother and me fight all the bloody time,' he says, looking directly into my eyes. And he is so close to me now I can't even turn my head to look at Florence for support. But at least I can still feel her holding my hand, and her face is also very close to mine. I can feel her warm breath sending tingles down my spine. He doesn't see her, but she sees him.

Florence and Giselle are two of the few people that I allow contact with. It can be too much to handle sometimes in the physical world. Even though I often wonder why I don't get hugged like other children, when someone does hug me I am reminded of what I am missing, what love is supposed to be. I don't like the feeling of being loved for one minute and then knowing what I am missing for the rest of the time. I'd almost rather never be loved for ever than know what I am missing. So, I try to keep my distance.

And the only regular physical contact I have with my father these days is when he transforms into the Enemy. When I was younger, we would play a game he called 'Tarzan and the tiger'. I would be Tarzan and he would be the tiger, and he would wrestle with me playfully, and pretend to try to eat me. This is my favourite memory, when he was still 'Dad', but then the fighting started, and he changed.

We have reached a crossroads on the stairs. I can see there is a chance he might calm down and change back into my father. But I must stay still and ride it out or the transition won't happen.

Sure enough, his anger starts to fade, and his self-awareness kicks in and forces him to assess his actions. Now his conscience is telling him to ask for forgiveness. Next thing he is wanting me to embrace and forgive him. For me, this is worse than the anger, this is more confusing than the spitting and shouting.

I'm given no time to protest as he imposes himself onto me, wrapping his arms around me and forcing me to embrace him back.

'You know I fucking love you, right?' he says, quietly. 'You just get me so mad when you act up.'

'It's fine,' I say, looking over at Florence. She knows it's not fine.

He pulls back so that he can see my face, and says, 'Tell me you love me.'

I guess I do love my father, but not the Enemy, so how do I tell him I love him without also telling his terrifying alter-ego? I also know that if I don't answer his question soon, I run the risk of undoing this moment of peace.

'I love you.'

He hears what he needs to hear to feel better about himself. He loosens his grip on me, and then goes to check I've put away my sister's dress and shoes that he caught me holding. He then walks back past me and into the kitchen, leaving me alone on the stairs with Florence. My face still has got spit on it and my arm is throbbing from where he grabbed me. I am also shivering slightly as I am still only wearing my underpants and vest.

'Do you think I could live in Domdie?' I ask Giselle. She and Florence are trying to warm me up. 'I don't think anyone would miss me if I left, I don't think I would miss anyone here, either.'

Florence puts her arms around me and says, 'You are always welcome and always present.'

'You're never not there when you are here,' confirms Giselle.

'I am not sure how much longer I can keep floating, before I drown,' I say.

And just like that, we're in Domdie. Giselle, Florence and I are in a dinghy boat, and with my hand I feel the cold smoothness of the water as it caresses my fingers. The sun is only just beginning to rise, so there hasn't been enough time to warm up the lake. I watch my hand dive in and resurface like a dolphin. Florence is sitting next to me, grasping the ropes for the sail as Giselle holds the rudder. Thankfully there is a slight breeze, just enough to fill the sails but not too much to generate waves, so we are gently flowing with the wind.

When I am in Domdie with my friends, there isn't a need to fill the silence, we can all happily enjoy the peace without interruption from pointless conversation. I find the real world so full of commotion and clamour that the real meaningful moments get lost. Maybe if my world were quieter, I could stay there longer without feeling the need to escape.

As our boat reaches a small island, Florence throws a rope and catches a nearby tree stump. She hands me the end of the rope and jumps from the boat, landing safely at the edge of the shallow water. With one hand she reaches out and takes back the rope, keeping our boat from drifting away. With her other hand, she reaches out for me.

'Jump to me,' she says.

I jump from the boat and land beside her. She takes my hand and leads me onto the island. We find ourselves standing in front of a castle, just like the one she'd stepped out of when we first met.

'Why are we here?' I ask.

She stops just outside the castle entrance, turns to me and with sadness in her voice she says:

'I don't want the mornings to feel sad anymore. I want to see you, I want to help you, protect you and love you. But I can't do all of that from here, so I need to say goodbye.'

We both stand still for a moment, looking at each other.

'I don't want you to go,' I say at last. My voice is cracking a little. I have never had to say goodbye to any of my invisible friends.

She puts her arms around me, and I can feel the tears breaking loose from my eyes and sliding down my face.

She pulls back slightly and says again, 'I don't think I can help you anymore, from here.'

'What do you mean?' I ask.

'I can't tell you the answers, because you need to find them out for yourself,' she continues.

'Where will you go?'

'I will find a way to become visible, to be with you in your world.'

'I still don't understand,' I say.

'It will make sense when the time comes, don't worry.'

And just like the moment I met her – but in reverse – she turns and walks back into the darkness. I am standing alone, trying to make sense of what just happened.

And then I am back on the staircase. I stand up from the step, feeling heartbroken and using the wall to help me back down to my bedroom.

Giselle is sitting on my bed, feeling bad about what happened with John. 'Maybe I shouldn't drive the skin machine anymore.'

It's true: when she takes over, it always gets us into trouble. But I like letting her take over, she is way more confident than I am, and it allows me to take a step back from the intensity of everyday life.

But right now, all I can think about is Florence. I am not sure how her leaving helps me, and I will miss her friendship and wisdom. It will feel strange not having her when I need help making hard choices. But I do believe in her, and for whatever reason she had to leave, I'm sure it was worth it, even though I might have to wait twenty years to find out what that worth is.

CHAPTER 12

Giving Up

1987 (age seven)

The sound of laughter from outside my window reaches me. My siblings are all out there, helping to pack the car for our boat holiday on the River Shannon, while I am in Ruth's bedroom upstairs, trying to be left behind. Wanting to be forgotten. My brother and sisters' happiness and excitement only makes me numb. I wish I could feel something, anything. Why can't I be happy?

It's a sunny bright May morning and school holidays begin in about a week's time, but my parents have taken us out of school early as usual to take advantage of the cheaper hire rates; the price to rent a boat on the River Shannon will be double next week, so the only way to get an affordable summer holiday for our family is to take these unconventional steps. I don't mind missing the last week of school, as one less week surrounded by the school bullies is a respite from the misery I'm experiencing there every day.

My parents are obsessed with boats and every summer for ten days we cram into the family car and drive the three hours from Dublin to Carrick-on-Shannon, a small town in Leitrim. I say a small town, but that is in relation to Dublin. Actually Carrick-on-Shannon is the largest town in the county of Leitrim, but Leitrim itself is the smallest county in the entire country. The town sits on a county border, so while I might be gathering supplies for the holiday in the local sweet shop, which is in Leitrim, my brother might be across the road in County Roscommon.

I used to look forward to these holidays. On these trips, my dad always remained calm, loving and fun. He never changed into the Enemy. Sometimes I wished we could live on the boat forever.

But this year feels different. All I can see is sadness in everything.

Mam is busy cooking two chickens before we go, to prepare meals for the week to save money, rather than us all eat out. I can hear her rushing into the kitchen, opening the oven and poking the chickens with a small metal rod, checking that they're cooking properly.

I'm wondering whether they'd notice if I didn't go with them. They might appreciate the extra space in the car. And Simon would get his own room on the boat too.

'Is everyone here?' John calls out, as he shuts the car boot.

'Yes!' shout Ruth, Simon and Leah at the same time.

I know I should get up, head outside and join them in the car, but I can't. There is something stopping me from moving, I feel like there is a darkness surrounding me and I don't see a way through it. This has got worse lately, and I think I've reached the point where it's starting to become hard to see any light anymore.

I hear the muffled voices of Ruth and Simon talking about what games they will play during the drive. Our favourite is the memory game. We always start with, 'I went to Dunnes Stores and I bought . . .' Dunnes Stores is an Irish supermarket, unique in regards to other supermarkets like Superquinn, Quinnsworth and Supervalue in that it doesn't only stock food; its large warehouse-like building is split into sections, including an area for home décor and even a space for clothing. This makes using Dunnes Stores the best choice for the game because of its variety.

Second to the memory game is the alphabet game, where you have to name things starting with the same letter, with categories such as boys' and girls' names, fruit, chocolate brands etc. This one always starts out with great enthusiasm, but as the categories get more obscure and the names became more creative, there will be more and more arguing, and this will cause Mam to turn around and slap the nearest pair of legs she can find. They are always mine as I sit in the middle with Ruth and Leah on one side and Simon on the other, who can lean into the safety of the door.

John calls out to Mam. He is frustrated because we haven't left already.

'Are you ready yet? Hurry up with those bloody chickens!'

The drive to Carrick is three hours, plus there will be the inevitable few stops along the way for toilet breaks, so the sooner we set off from the house, the further down the river he can get and really kickstart the holiday.

'Where the fuck is Jonathan?' I hear him ask angrily, realising I am not in the car.

I know I should be scared enough to go down the stairs and join them, but I am empty, devoid of all feelings. Maybe if he turns into the Enemy and attacks me, I will feel something. I always want to feel less and now that I do, it's almost worse. Maybe feeling nothing isn't enough to stop feeling nothing.

I realise I am now sitting on the window ledge. I'm not sure how or why I've made that move. I am only a few metres above him, but I say nothing.

Mam comes bursting into the room.

'What are you doing? Come on!' she says anxiously. 'Your father is getting angry.'

But I don't respond. I can hear her, but I don't have any words to express myself.

I just stay motionless, emotionless.

Getting frustrated with my lack of response she approaches me, but I still don't move, I don't even acknowledge her.

This seems to strike her dumb for a moment, something quite rare for my mam, as she always has words for every occasion. Instead, she sits down next to me on the window ledge where I am hunched over and puts her hand on my leg.

'Jonathan,' she says gently, using her hand to turn my face around her so that she can look into my eyes. 'What's wrong?'

'Nothing,' I reply, quietly. 'Nothing is wrong.' After a long pause, I add, 'But nothing is right either.'

'What do you mean?' she asks.

I look right at her; I don't have tears in my eyes because they have run out a long time ago. I remember crying when I was younger and then being comforted, but then in the last year or so, whenever I cry no one comforts me, no one even sees my tears, so I have taught myself to turn off the tap.

'I don't want to live here anymore,' I say.

'Don't be silly, this is our home, where do you want to live?' she says in a jokey tone.

'No, not here as in our house, here as in *this world*,' I reply. 'If I can't be me, I can't be happy, so what's the point. Everyone gets so mad at me all the time, and I don't know how to be what they want me to be.'

I don't want to tell her about my state of mind, but she asked. I don't want to make other people feel sorry for me, I don't want my sadness to become infectious, even to the Enemy I live with, and the bullies I am at school with. I don't wish them my sadness.

I'm also conscious of the fact that if I share my sadness then maybe too, I have to share my Domdie, and I don't want to do that. It is my place to hide from my pain, where I can be energised and renewed. I can't risk losing it.

Mam stands up and leaves the room. She walks down the stairs and out to the car, which has been manoeuvred during our conversation so that it is pointing in the direction of the road, ready to depart. I can hear her talking to John about me.

'He isn't happy, John, something is really wrong.'

'Something is always wrong with him, just get him in the car,' he replies, impatiently.

She comes back to me, where I am still sitting in the same spot. She leans down to me, so that she is at the same eye level.

'Don't leave without talking to me first, okay?' she says. 'Promise me.'

I don't like lying, but people don't like my truth, so they force me to lie to suit them.

They say, 'You won't get in trouble if you tell the truth, Jonathan', so I tell the truth and I am told my truth is wrong. My experience of life is flawed apparently, so I have learnt it's best to go along with whatever people expect from me.

'Okay,' I say, 'I won't go anywhere.'

We get up and leave my bedroom together. I let Mam walk out of the front door first and use her as a shield in case the Enemy is waiting for me. As I open the car door, I can tell everyone is frustrated with me.

Mam breaks the silence.

'Have you got something to say to everyone?' she asks, wanting to put an end to this drama so that the holiday can well and truly begin.

'Sorry,' I say.

John starts driving, and far too fast.

'We have no time for this bullshit,' he says to nobody in particular. He takes a right onto Fortfield Road, and then a left down Wainsford Road, and up to the Templogue round-about, when suddenly:

'The chickens!' Mam exclaims. 'I've left them in the oven!'

John swerves as he abandons the roundabout exit he was about to take and goes back 'round in the direction we just came from.

'Aaaagh, for fuck's sake!' he shouts.

Back down Wainsford Road, right onto Fortfield Road and then back into the driveway. The car hasn't even stopped, and Mam has already jumped out and unlocked the front door.

John turns to look at me.

'You know whose fault this is, right?' He sounds so angry.

I guess I had distracted Mam so much with the shock of my truth that she ended up forgetting the chickens. How will this ever change? My lies get me in trouble, my truth gets me in trouble.

'Open the boot,' says Mam as she runs to the car holding a cooked chicken in each hand. But the boot is completely packed with not even enough space for two small cooked chickens.

'Right,' she says as she passes the chickens through the window and into the back of the car. 'You'll have to hold these, and don't eat any.'

She gets back into the car, and off we go again.

'I wish Florence was still here,' I say. 'She would know what to do.'

'Who is Florence?' asks Leah.

I stare at Leah. I am completely shocked as to how she heard me. Is Leah like me? She is only five, but then again, I'd already made quite a few invisible friends by her age. I don't know what to say so I stare back out of the window in the hope that she gives up.

'Is that your brain's name?' laughs Simon, who has grasped this opportunity to tease me. 'Flynner's brain is called Florence!' he chants as I keep my eyes fixed on the blurred passing trees.

It turns out that I have said 'I wish Florence was still here' out loud by mistake, and because Leah is squashed in the middle with me, she overheard me. I realise I am finding it harder and harder not to talk to them out loud.

Only a week before, during our annual dentist trip, I was caught out. My mam picked Simon and me up from Terenure with two school uniforms from the local non-fee-paying school, St Joseph's. My mam does a great job at making sure we look the part, living in the right road, attending the right school with the right friends, but it is all a pretence because we aren't from those privileged backgrounds. When it comes to things like a dental check-up there isn't any money to pay for it, so she finds ways around the system to make sure we get the opportunities. So that's why we were now disguised in our non-fee-paying school uniforms, having swapped our

Terenure College ones for them. She knows that having our teeth seen to is a free public service offered to those that are means tested and do not pass the threshold.

But on this occasion her ploy backfires.

While in the car waiting for our appointment slot, she runs though the script of answers we need to remember just in case someone asks us questions.

'What school do you attend?' she quickly asked both of us.

'St Joseph's,' Simon replied with confidence.

'Very good,' she said. 'And what is your teacher's name, Jonathan?'

'Erm, Miss . . . O'Shea?' I replied, with much less confidence than Simon.

'No!' exclaims Mam. 'That was your Low Babies teacher, they will know that's not right.'

'Sorry,' I say.

The problem is, while she was running through all the questions and answers, I wasn't paying attention. I was drifting between Domdie and here, I had just come from another brutal day in the life of Jonathan at Terenure College, so concentrating was a little difficult.

Mam ran though the answers one more time and then we headed into the dentist's practice.

This is where it's hard to explain yourself to a system that judges you on appearances. You might look one way, but really you are another. I always found it amusing that my life was a perfect representation of this very fact, yet I was never allowed to show what I actually looked like behind the projection. I just learnt my rehearsed answers that led to little resistance and when no one was looking, I could be myself.

The surgery was a makeshift faded blue prefab in a car park on the high street, with two plastic windows at the front, and two at the back. There was only enough seating for maybe four people at a time in the waiting-room, so if it was a busy period you would have to wait outside. On this visit the waiting room was completely empty so there was enough room for us all to sit.

Simon was going to be up first, so I picked up a magazine from the table. The magazine was almost bigger than my head, so when I held it up I couldn't see anything over it. This suited me fine because I was always looking for ways to hide myself whenever I was uncomfortable which, to be honest, was most of the time. The dentist came out to meet Simon and asked Mam to come with them to show her an Xray. I was left alone looking at the pictures in my magazine, when suddenly I heard laughter. I lowered the page slowly. Sitting in the remaining empty chairs were Giselle, Florence and someone else I didn't know.

They were full of smiles, amused by the difference between my tiny body and the large magazine. We laughed quietly, sharing this in-joke, and I forgot where I was for a moment. Then I suddenly remembered I'd forgotten all the answers I was meant to give if I was asked about my school.

'Do you remember the answers to Mam's questions to give to the dentist?' I said out loud, something I would do when I thought no one would hear me.

And then a voice from across the room responded.

'What was that, my dear?' It came from behind a desk I hadn't noticed before. There was a receptionist in the room with me, but I hadn't seen her as she was sitting behind a stack of files and books. She stood up the better to hear me, just as Mam was coming into the room.

'What questions or answers are you talking about?' she asked, slightly confused.

My mam's eyes darted from the receptionist to me and back to the receptionist.

'What was that?' she asked, and I could hear the tension in her voice.

'He asked whether I remembered the answers to his mam's questions,' the receptionist said with a cautious tone, looking back at Mam.

I didn't know what to say. I had completely forgotten my

rehearsed lines so if I was about to be questioned, I would certainly fail. And it looked like I'd landed Mam in it too.

There was a silent stand-off between the three of us as we all waited for someone to say something. Then one of the answers popped into my head.

'I go to Presentation!' I announced to the room, which was the wrong answer on several fronts, as I should have said St Joseph's and also there was no way I could still be going to Presentation, because all the boys are kicked out after first class.

Mam was sending me looks that could kill, the receptionist was sending me looks of confusion and then Simon burst through the door and broke the deadlock.

'You're up, Flynner,' he said loudly as he walked over to where I was sitting.

I got up, walked past the receptionist and then past Mam, making my best effort to avoid eye contact with them, and headed inside the dentist's room. I hopped up onto the chair, put on the glasses and waited for the dentist to begin his inspection of my mouth.

'That was close,' I said to Giselle. I knew I should be worrying more about whether my mother would be found out, but I was more concerned about people knowing why I was talking out loud.

This is what is going through my head in the car on the way to the River Shannon: it's getting harder all the time to hide my invisible friends. Things are feeling like they are exploding. I don't know what's next but for the moment my head is full of question marks and fear.

CHAPTER 13

Underneath My Clothes

1988 (age eight)

It's been a few months now since Florence left, and I feel like there is an emptiness in my life. The once strong voice of reason has been replaced with silence. Giselle tries to offer guidance, but her voice is my voice, and between us we don't have a great track record of making good choices. We always lead with our heart and our emotions and it's those very things that bring out the Enemy. Whereas Florence led with her brain and logic and reasoning, and that is what we need to balance things out.

I am sitting in the passenger seat of my mam's car. She has decided to bring me with her for a Big Talk while she is travelling for work. Although it's been a while since the day we left for the River Shannon, I think she is still a bit shaken by me telling her I don't want to be here anymore, and now she is worried about leaving me alone. I don't mind, as being at home means there is a greater chance the Enemy will find me. The car has stopped at the checkpoint at the border to the North, so it must be time for us to get out.

'No messing, Jonathan,' she says in her serious voice, like she always does when we approach officials.

'I know,' I reply, rolling my eyes.

It's the same routine whenever I accompany my mam to Newry, in County Armagh, Northern Ireland, where my mam sometimes works. It's about sixty miles from Dublin. The Irish-British border runs from Lough Foyle in the north of Ireland to Carlingford Lough in the northeast, separating the Republic of Ireland from Northern Ireland. This was established in 1921, and as it's still a few years before the European Union will be formed in 1993 (making travel across the border no issue), Mam needs to let the British military check our car as we cross over to make sure we're not with the IRA and carrying any bombs.

A British solider holding a rifle in both hands approaches and signals to us that we must step out of the car so that it can be inspected. I know Giselle is with me, but I still feel very anxious during this routine inspection. I reach over slowly to open my door. As the cold air from outside passes over me, I feel my body react and shiver, but I must remain calm and collected, and continue to keep eye contact with this giant of a man standing in front of me. I don't want to seem like I have anything to hide or give him any reason to use his weapon.

'Hello there, wee fella,' he says in his Northern Irish accent as he lowers his weapon. 'How are you doing?'

I am glad he recognises me as a friend and not an enemy, which means he is not an enemy either. I am well aware of how enemies can hide in plain sight. It would be a lot easier if the baddies were obvious like in movies and comics, but in reality I usually can't tell the difference until it's too late. And that is probably why, every time we pass through a border checkpoint, the soldier approaches the car with his rifle pointed at us, unsure of our intentions. It must be hard for them to tell who the baddies are, too.

I walk over and stand beside my mother as we wait for them to do their checks, first using a mirror to look under the car for concealed devices, and then inspecting the inside.

The metal walls surrounding the checkpoint seem as high as the sky, and a helicopter hovers above us. There is a long queue of cars waiting their turn, and an equally long queue of people like us standing out in the cold, next to the giant walls, hoping to be let through.

169

'You do know what I am saying, right?' Mam says to me, continuing the conversation we were having before we arrived at the checkpoint. 'I don't want you to always be the victim; if you just acted more like them, they would accept you as one of their own, and maybe they would stop picking on you.'

I look up at her and I have to squint because the sun's rays are finding gaps between the clouds and they are blinding me. Instead, I look at Giselle and reply to her as if I am talking to my mam.

'Why do I have to pretend to be like them, just to stop them from hitting me?' I ask.

There is a long pause, and just as Mam is about to answer me, the soldier waves us over and tells us we can be on our way.

Mam drives off out of the checkpoint and back onto the Newry road. In Northern Ireland, the roads are better and with no potholes, and we are about to join the motorway.

I think a lot about Mam's advice, which echoes what Florence said too about pretending and adapting. Maybe they are both right.

A few days later, we are back at home and I am getting ready for school. As I reach for the girls' socks I keep hidden down the side of my bed, Giselle takes hold of my hand.

'Leave the socks,' she says. 'Let's do something new.'

As ever, she can read my mind, and she wants to help me give the pretence of being 'normal' a go and make it more bearable.

I sneak into my sisters' room while they and the rest of the family are downstairs in the kitchen, having breakfast and getting ready to leave for school. It's easy to find what I need, as there isn't an abundance of toys or clothes in their bedroom, there just isn't the money. I quickly find the treasure I am after. I pull open the top drawer, reach in and grab a pair of Ruth's underwear.

'Do you like these?' I ask Giselle. They are yellow with a small pink flower in the centre and white stitching along the edges. She smiles and nods, so I quickly sneak back to my room, pull them on and conceal them under my grey school trousers. I slip on my black school shoes. I turn and look in the mirror at us.

'We look just like the other boys, so maybe this will work,' I say.

That morning at school I feel like Giselle and I have a physical connection on the outside of my body as well as on the inside. Maybe I have found a way to be both Giselle *and* like the boys around me.

The other boys and I wait in our classroom for the arrival

of the teacher for our maths lessons. This is usually the most dangerous part of my school day, when I am surrounded by unsupervised wolves. It always begins with a whisper and then the noise grows and spreads around the room as I become the centre of the joke. Even the boys who wouldn't usually be mean but who know it's them or me, will also join in. But this morning feels different; their jokes hurt a little less because now Giselle isn't just invisible, we are united in our skin machine. And it makes me feel confident.

When the bell rings as the class ends, I feel relief to have survived another lesson. Not only that, but to have survived together, Giselle and me. Maybe this is the way I can do what my mam suggests. I can be more like the other boys on the outside, where everyone sees me, but on the inside, hidden underneath, I can be myself.

'If this works out maybe I don't have to leave this world,' I say to Giselle as I stand up from my desk and begin to gather my things. 'Maybe I could just pretend to be like them when I am with other people,' I continue excitedly, thinking I might have just found a solution to my identity problem. 'Maybe Mam was right.'

'Mr Williamson will meet you all outside,' announces the teacher as he leaves the room.

There must be a rugby game on or something, I think as I

grab my bag. *Why else would we be told to wait outside?* And then it dawns on me. As I lift the bag up, I can see a towel sticking out of the top and that means only one thing: it is swimming day, and I am about to be in a room with thirty other boys, and we will be undressing together. I can't believe I have been so stupid as to forget.

We arrive at the pool, which is inside the school grounds and just a two-minute walk from the main school building. Mr Williamson is escorting us there, so there is no opportunity for me to hide and wait out the lesson. I listen to all the other boys excitedly chatting away to each other about whatever it is boys chat about. They can't hear me talk away to my invisible friends about our interests, but I am confident that if the boys were to overhear us, it would result in humiliation.

The entrance to the swimming pool is a faded brown door with nearly opaque plastic windows. As the door opens, the smell of chorine rushes over me. It always reminds me of Mam, it has become part of her essence. Inside the door is a small waiting area with a large window into the main pool. On either side of the glass are two doors: one the boys' changing rooms and one for the girls' – even though this is a boys' school, the swimming-pool is used by others outside school hours. As we wait to change, I can hear some of the boys waiting outside laughing and talking about me.

'Hey, Joly, you're in the wrong line,' says one of them, while the others laugh along.

I know I shouldn't respond but before I have time to process that, I already have.

'We're all in the same line,' I say defensively.

'But shouldn't you be in the other line?' someone shouts, pointing over to the girls' changing room.

I turn back around, facing away from them in the hope they will get bored without a reaction from me, but at the same time I fantasise about walking over to the girls' changing room and entering. I've been inside it before, and I know that it's all painted pink, unlike the dull colour of the boys' one.

We are ushered into the boys' changing room, where there are ten small changing cubicles lining the left wall, and on the right side is a bench running the length of the room. My only hope is to get into one of the private spaces so I can hide my perversion.

As I enter, I notice the class before us has already claimed the small changing cubicles and the only option is the bench. So instead of taking a seat I head straight to the toilet and lock myself inside one of the stalls. Sitting on the toilet, I take off my trousers and then pull down my sister's underwear.

'How does something like this cause so many problems?' I say, holding the soft yellow fabric in my hands. 'I don't think I can be the pretender Mam wants me to be.'

There is a tiny little window high above the toilet, which I can reach if I stand on the toilet seat, so I wrap the underwear into a little ball as small as I can and climb up. Standing on my tippy toes, I manage to stuff it through the window. And just like that, the evidence is gone, but so too is my physical connection to Giselle. I am once again on my own and she is once again invisible. This will leave me with no underwear for the rest of the day, but I think that's better than getting caught and having to live through it.

I head back into the changing area and find a space to put my bag down. Most of the boys are all changed at this point, so I begin to undress. I pull off my shoes and place them under the bench, and then slide off my socks and place them inside my shoes. I take a little look around to make sure no one is looking and then I pull down my trousers. Patrick is the first to notice I have no underwear on, and he begins to laugh.

'Lads, look! Joly doesn't have any jocks on!' he exclaims. And the whole room starts laughing.

'I forgot to put them on,' I say, embarrassed.

'How do you forget to put on your pants?' someone shouts.

'Freak!' exclaims someone else.

And then everybody starts chanting: 'Joly's got no jocks, Joly's got no jocks!'

The sound of the chanting and cheering capture the attention of Mr Williamson as he enters the changing room. 'What is going on here? Keep it down, gents,' he says in his slightly angry but still upbeat and friendly tone.

'Sir, Joly isn't wearing any underwear,' announces Patrick.

Mr Williamson looks over at me as I am standing wearing only my jumper and shirt, completely exposed down below. He walks over to me and stands right in front of me. Shaking his head, he says, 'Cop on to yourself.'

The room descends into laughter again as they have just been given permission to continue their mockery at my expense.

'Sorry, Sir,' I say. 'I will try not to forget again.'

He shakes his head and turns his back on me, facing the room. There is a further outburst from the boys – he has clearly made a facial expression for only them to see.

I feel my body become weightless as I close my eyes and let my legs lose power and retract. I am sitting back down on the bench, but I don't end up on a bench, instead I land on a fallen tree. The sound of my classmates' laughter begins to fade and as I feel the bark on my naked skin, I open my eyes to find I am no longer in the swimming pool changing room, I am back in the safety of Domdie. My anxiety is disappearing with my hopelessness. I turn to see my friends waiting for me to join them by the swings.

'You go and play,' says Giselle. 'I will look after us in the real world.' I run off as Giselle takes control of our body. She gets dressed into our swimming clothes, ignoring all the noise surrounding us and walks out to the pool side.

I find I am relying on Giselle more and more to take the driver's seat of our skin machine when situations like these arise. She can somehow turn off her emotions or maybe she just manages them better. When she is in control, we feel stronger, we feel more brave and less afraid of this world, but sadly this isn't sustainable, and I will have to regain operational control soon. Therefore, I don't see any way for us to remain here. The short breaks are a nice pause but it's getting to the point where it's no longer enough. I miss being in Domdie more than I like being here.

CHAPTER 14

The Lost Bag

1988 (age eight)

I start skiving off school.

The first time I missed a lesson, it went a bit wrong. I left without being noticed and hid in a small, wooded area called St Anne's near our house. I had brought a bag of clothes with me – a collection of Ruth's clothes that I'd been pinching for months.

'Fashion show!' exclaimed Giselle, as I hung the bag from a low hanging branch.

'The only problem is that we don't have a mirror,' I said. 'We won't be able to see ourselves.'

'What about a car window?' suggested Giselle. 'There are a few parked just at the entrance of the woods.'

We decided to try on the red dress first. The dress was simple but pretty, it had two large white flowers spread across the front.

I took off my school uniform and piled it up next to the tree. I pulled the dress over my head.

'What do you think?' I asked Giselle. The soft cotton felt nice against my skin.

'I don't know yet,' she replied. 'Let's check at a car.'

We made our way over to the edge of the trees and peeked out to check if anyone was around. The coast was clear, so we stepped out from behind the trees and stood on the little brick wall surrounding the carpark, which meant we could see our reflection in the car window. Thankfully the window was clean, it looked like the car had just been washed, so not only did we get a glass window reflection, but we also got a full body view.

We struck poses and moved around as if we were models on a catwalk.

'Stunning,' said Giselle.

'If only we were allowed to let our hair grow, we would look so pretty,' I replied as we admired ourselves.

Distracted by our own reflection, we hadn't noticed a man approaching from the estate around the corner. By the time we saw him, it was too late: there was nowhere to hide other than by running back into the woods. But surely seeing an eight-year-old boy dressed as a girl dashing towards the trees would cause concern?

'Hello,' said the man as he walked past.

We just froze in fear.

'You look great,' he said, as he continued walking.

We looked at each other, unsure as to what had just happened.

'Was he invisible?' I whispered to Giselle.

'I don't think so,' she replied, 'but he obviously had a good eye for fashion.'

Buoyed by the stranger's comment, we skipped back into the woods with a newfound sense of confidence, keen to try on another dress. We pulled down the bag from the tree and dug around inside.

'I can't decide, they're all my favourites,' I said.

'Pity we can't wear them all the time,' said Giselle. 'And it's such a shame that, as that man said, we look great, and yet we only ever get to do this when we are hiding.'

'At least it's not like before, when we didn't have our own collection,' I replied.

And then we heard a car door close, and another. The sound was coming from just outside the woods. We heard a man's voice.

'Hello?'

I wondered if it was that man again. We leaned around the tree to get a better look. But it wasn't, it was two men, dressed in head to toe in blue, each with a radio in his hand. It was the Gardai.

'Change back quickly!' hushed Giselle. 'Don't get caught like this.'

We pulled off the red dress and stuffed it back into the bag, and swiftly got the Terenure uniform back on just as the two officers came into full view.

'What are you doing in here, son?' asked one of the men as he approached.

'Playing,' I replied.

'Are you not supposed to be in school?' he asked.

'Use your Terenure lingo,' Giselle suggested. 'He will let you off if he thinks you're a good Terenure boy.'

I straightened up.

'It's a half day, Sir,' I said, adding in the Sir to present myself well.

The officer then noticed the bag on the ground.

'Is this your bag?' he asked, pointing to my collection.

'No, Sir,' I said. 'I don't know what that is. I sometimes just play here after school.'

The man looked at me closely.

'We got a call from a lady across the road saying there

was some suspicious activity happening over here,' he announced.

'I didn't see anything,' I said quickly and confidently so that it didn't look like I was part of any suspicious activity.

'Where do you live?' he asked, getting a pad and pen out.

'Give him a fake address,' urged Giselle.

'Fortfield Road, Sir,' I replied, too nervous to tell any more lies.

He paused for a moment and reached down to grab the bag. My heart sank but I couldn't protest.

'Go on home, son, and don't play here anymore, okay? It's private property.'

'Sorry, Sir,' I said as I made my way out of the woods and headed across the road to the lane that led back to my street.

I looked back from a safe distance and watched as the two gardai opened the bag and took out the clothes They held them up, one by one, clearly curious as to why they were there in the woods. As hard as it was to give them up, I also felt exonerated – they would never believe I'd been trying them on. After all, why would a boy have a bag of girl's clothes?

It was a close shave, so now when I skip swimming, I go for a walk with my invisible friends instead, and don't do anything to draw attention. And I am also very careful to not arouse suspicion at home. It's all about the small details.

At first, I would get caught out because I would leave my dry towel and swimming trucks in my bag, a big red flag for my mam. Such giveaway clues are easily forgotten during the adrenaline rush that comes when escaping from the lesson.

So now, before I go home, I sneak into the gym next to the pool, and step fully clothed into the mosaic-tiled shower cubicle. I press the button for the water and quickly pull myself back before the shower fully bursts into life. I then lean into the water and get my hair soaked, careful not to get my clothes wet. I also wave my towel and trunks under the stream for a quick moment, so when I get home later, all the signs that I went to swimming will be there.

When I leave the gym, it's late afternoon and the sun has already set, so under the cover of darkness, I begin walking away.

'We should probably go the long way around, in case a car comes,' suggests Giselle, who is being surprisingly practical.

There is only one entrance to the pool from the main road, and if I am seen walking up the driveway alone, someone will probably stop or even say something.

'Good idea,' I say.

'See, Abigail, I sometimes do have good ideas,' says Giselle with a hint of sass.

'That's because getting it right takes a lot of getting it wrong,' replies Abigail with authority.

We make it out the of the gate and onto Templeville Road without been seen. We then take a left and head to the roundabout, but before we get that far we turn left down Wainsford Crescent to avoid being exposed on the main road and risk being caught.

We turn into College Park which is a quiet road. It is very unlikely someone will see us here, as there are no lights. The only light that illuminates the path comes from one of the houses set back from the road, but it's far enough away that it doesn't trouble us.

This road leads me to St Pius' Church, where I was christened. It's a nice spot to hang out alone with my invisible friends and listen to the music coming from the choir singing inside and the large organ that accompanies it.

'Hide!' Giselle suddenly shouts.

Without a moment's hesitation, I step into the nearest garden to avoid finding myself in the beams of the car. The closer the car gets, the more I can see that it seems to be exactly like my father's Mazda 323. The car slows down as it reaches me, and I can see the driver is indeed John. He pulls over.

I wonder what he is doing here. Unless you live here, you

wouldn't really drive down this road. Does he know I'm here? Has he been told I've disappeared?

I assume someone has called him, and ready myself to step out of the shadows when I see a woman I don't recognise appear on the path close by. She walks up to his side of the car. They talk for less than a minute before she walks around and gets into the passenger seat.

'Is that Mam?' asks Giselle tentatively.

'I don't think so,' I reply. 'Mam doesn't have blonde hair.'

The car drives off and the darkness returns.

'That was lucky,' says Abigail.

'We still have some time before we need to be home,' says Giselle. 'Let's go see if the choir is singing.'

'Okay,' I reply, looking back to where my father's taillights have disappeared into the darkness, trying to understand what I have just witnessed.

We walk in the direction of St Pius' Church.

As we approach, we hear beautiful voices from inside.

'Sail away, sail away, sail away,' they sing.

I think about how nice it would be to sail away.

'Let's sail to Domdie,' says Giselle, who can always read my thoughts.

I just smile back as her, and we listen to the rest of the song together before making our way home.

CHAPTER 15

A New Hope

1989 (age nine)

I need to explain to Giselle how I feel. I need her to know that I'm finding it harder to be in both places at once. Sometimes I even get confused as to where I am and where I'm supposed to be. I'm scared of losing her if I'm in one world and she's in another. I need to make sure she'll never leave me.

When I tell her about this, I am sitting with Mam in Father Kilmurray's office. We are sitting on an uncomfortable wooden chair, and we are in an uncomfortable situation. Mam has been called into school for a meeting; they have concerns about me and feel like they have reached a point of no return.

That's when I ask Giselle to always be me.

'Of course!' smiles Giselle reassuringly. And she puts her

hand on my mine. 'Always,' she promises. 'No matter which world you're in, I will be you always.'

I feel my mother squeeze my other hand. She wants me to pay attention. I tune in to what Father Kilmurray is saying.

'I just don't think it's fair on Jonathan, or on his classmates. We've tried a number of methods to solve his problems, to correct his behaviour, but nothing seems to be working,' he continues, glancing from me to Mam.

'I don't want to give up on him,' replies Mam.

'But the money you are paying for him to be here is in vain,' he answers. 'Why not send him to a non-fee-paying school, where he can wait out his time? He's not learning anything here anyway, and I haven't seen him making any friends either.'

'There must be another option,' Mam pleads. 'There must be somewhere we can send him, for kids like him. I don't want him to just fade into the background, sit in some classroom and wait out his life.' She sounds almost emotional, which isn't like her.

There is a long silence, and then Father Kilmurray says, 'There might be one option, but I don't think he will see you.'

I look at Father Kilmurray, at my Mam, and then at Father Kilmurray again. Who is this person who could save me, and who won't see me?

'Who?' asks Mam.

'There is this Jesuit priest, Father Andrews,' he answers as he ruffles through some paper on his desk. 'He is doing some experiments, a trial of sorts for children like Jonathan. Children who are, shall we say, different. But, like I said, I don't think you will be able to get a meeting with him.'

Giselle has something to say to me. 'I don't think he knows who he is talking to,' she says. 'If there is anyone who will do a thing when they are told they can't, it will be our mam.'

Sure enough, my mother keeps making it clear she's not going to give up. 'How do I find this Father Andrews?' she asks with determination.

Father Kilmurray sighs.

'Even if you get to talk to him, or even see him, there will be a number of tests they will want to carry out, and an observation. So, the chances of Jonathan getting a place are still very unlikely, but we will support you if this is what you want.'

He hands her a sheet of paper with Father Andrews' information written down and we leave his office. Mam has that tone in her voice like a new mission is just beginning for her as she tells me to keep up. It's in the stride of her walk as well. No one else cares enough about me to even try, but she does. The same person who is sometimes an enemy too, who terrifies me just as much as my father when she's really angry, might be the one who will save me in the end.

A few weeks later, Mam has called St Declan's, the school that Father Andrews runs for children like me. They try to brush her off, but she has the bit between her teeth now. This conversation is always the same. She speaks to a receptionist called Karen, leaves her message for Father Andrews, and finishes with, 'Thanks, Karen, talk to you tomorrow.'

She never gives up.

Eventually the school realises this crazy woman will never stop calling until she gets her meeting, so it is agreed that Father Andrews will meet me – just for an informal chat, nothing official.

Mam has called Father Kilmurray so that I can have the day off school, but also to show him that she has achieved the thing he said she wouldn't. The drive to Ballsbridge is about twenty minutes from our house, and we park near the school on Northumberland Road. I am excited because I get to stay out of Terenure for a day.

'This doesn't look like a school,' observes Giselle, as we walk through the black metal gates.

'It looks like a house,' I agree.

I've only known schools to be imposing, like Presentation and Terenure, but this really is just a house on a road of houses, with windows with curtains and a red front door with a large gold handle in the centre. We walk up the concrete steps and ring the bell.

'Are you sure this isn't the bold boys' school?' worries Giselle.

'This seems way too nice,' I reply.

Suddenly Giselle squeals with excitement. 'Look over there!'

At the top of the stairs, we have a view over the wall that separates the house from the garden. And from our vantage point we can see that there are girls playing in the school's garden.

There are no words for this moment. Instead, Giselle squeezes my hand, letting me know what I have already decided.

We need to come here, we both think.

The door slowly opens, and a friendly-looking woman is standing there. She smiles at us both.

'Hello, Brid, I'm Karen,' she says like they're long-lost friends. 'Come in, won't you take a seat?'

We step inside the door.

Everything about this school is different to all the others I've been to – not just the outside. There is a warmth to the air, a calmness I haven't felt before. It is like being at my father's parents' house, the only escape I have in the real world, the only place I can go to and not be worried.

'Would you like a cup of tea, Brid?' asks Karen like they are old friends.

'Yes please, Karen,' replies Mam.

This all feels too good to be true. 'Are we in Domdie?' I ask Giselle, thinking this might be some kind of dream world, and that in a moment, I will wake up.

'No, this is real,' she replies.

We don't have to wait long before we are called up to meet Father Andrews.

'He would like to meet Jonathan first, if that's okay with you,' Karen says to Mam. 'He likes to observe without any distraction. It's completely normal.'

My mother nods and looks down at me: 'Try not to mess this up,' she whispers. I stand up from my chair.

'You can join him in a minute,' adds Karen.

I follow Karen out of the door, without Mam.

Father Andrews' office is on the third floor of the building, and as I follow Karen up the first flight of stairs, I glance into a classroom through the open door. There are only six or seven children in the class and half of them are girls. There are thirty boys and no girls in my class at Terenure.

We climb the next flight of stairs to the office.

'Hello,' Karen calls out as she knocks on the door. 'I've got Jonathan here.'

I hear a warm elderly voice respond. 'Come in, come in.'

Karen pushes the door open, and I walk in. A man with white hair and small glasses is standing just there. He is dressed in black and he has a white collar.

'Take a seat,' he says to me, adding, 'Thanks, Karen.' She leaves us to it.

There is a long sofa running the length of the wall at the back of the room, and a small desk and a filing cabinet on the other side. I sit on the sofa. The office has a large window looking out onto the back garden.

'So, Jonathan,' he says. 'How are you?' He takes a seat in his desk chair, opposite the sofa.

'Fine,' I reply, looking everywhere but at him. He seems very nice, but I have learnt to be wary of priests after my experiences at Terenure.

'I heard you might be having a hard time in school,' he says gently.

'Should we trust him?' I ask Giselle.

'I don't know yet,' she replies.

Father Andrews gets back up again and walks towards me. He hands me a small toy cow.

'Do you like animals?' he asks.

Suddenly, Abigail is here too. 'You have nothing to lose,' she says to me, encouragingly. So I look at Father Andrews and decide to trust him.

'Yes,' I say. 'I like animals more than people.'

'Why's that, then?' he asks.

'Well, animals are never mean to me,' I respond. 'But people are mean to them, and I think they are misunderstood, and never heard, and that's how I feel.'

'Interesting,' says Father Andrews. 'Do you like drawing?' He reaches over for a pad of paper and a box of colouring pencils.

'I guess,' I reply.

'Can you draw me your family?' He hands me the paper and pencils.

I'm confused. I've never drawn my family before. 'How should I draw them?' I ask.

'Just draw them however you want, however you see them,' he replies.

As I draw away on the pad of paper, we continue talking. He asks me about my friendships, my parents, my home life, what I like and don't like. It doesn't feel like an interview, more like talking to one of my invisible friends, which isn't something I am used to in the real world, especially with an adult.

Giselle is looking over my shoulder at my picture. 'I look great,' she says, pointing to the paper.

'I'm done,' I say as I hand him the picture.

He takes the paper, pulls down the small glasses that had been resting on his head, and examines my drawing.

'So, tell me about this drawing,' he says. 'Who's this?' he asks, pointing at my brother.

'That's Simon,' I reply.

'And this?'

'Ruth, holding Leah's hand, she likes to pretend Leah is her baby.'

'And this is Mam and Dad, right?" he says, as he points at my parents, who are standing next to Simon, Ruth and Leah in the picture.

'Yes, that's Mam and John,' I confirm.

'Mam and John, not Mam and Dad?' he says, as if to make sure.

'I don't know, yeah . . . That's what I call him, it's his name,' I say.

'Interesting,' he says again. He then points at the illustration I've made of myself. I'm standing on the other side of the page.

'Now, who is this, over here?' he asks.

'That's me,' I reply. It seems obvious to me.

'Why aren't you with your family?'

'I am,' I answer. I nod towards the little girl holding my hand I drew next to me.

'So, is this your family?' he asks, pointing to her.

'Yeah,' I reply.

'That's me!' says Giselle.

'Interesting.'

There is a knock on the door, Karen has brought my mam up. I am told that I'm going to follow Karen back down and wait there. At that moment a phone starts ringing in one of the other offices, and Karen asks me to wait for her just outside the door while she goes to answer the call. She doesn't quite close the door.

'Listen in,' says Giselle, pointing back inside towards Father Andrews' office.

'What if we get caught?' I ask.

'It's the only way to know if we are safe,' she says.

I step forwards and point my ear towards the door. I am well trained for this type of covert operation after years of Enemy evasion training. Sure enough, I can hear their conversation.

'He's an interesting boy,' Father Andrews says to Mam. 'How was your pregnancy with him?'

Why is he asking her about how it was when I was in her tummy, I wonder?

'Normal,' she replies. 'I was a nurse before I had children, so I would have known if there were any complications.'

'Anyone else like Jonathan in the family?' he asks.

'No, not that I am aware of,' she replies.

There is a pause. I can sense that Father Andrews is collecting his thoughts and about to make his decision.

'If I did work with Jonathan, there would be a number of rules that he and frankly the whole family would have to abide by,' he warns. 'Do you think that would be manageable?'

'Certainly,' she answers.

'How is your marriage?' he asks next.

'Karen's coming!' whispers Abigail just at that moment, and I move away from the door quickly and pretend that I've just been daydreaming all this time. We go back down to the waiting-room.

It doesn't take too long before Mam comes back down the stairs with Father Andrews.

'Karen,' he announces, winking at me at the same time. 'We're going to take on Jonathan.'

'Does that mean we don't have to go back to Terenure ever again?' asks Giselle, excitedly.

'I think so,' I reply. I hardly dare believe it myself. This is incredible. Giselle claps her hands.

'It's going to be just like before, with Grace and Gemma and everyone else!' she says.

'He will be starting in September,' I hear Father Andrews say to Mam and Karen.

My heart sinks a little.

'I think that means we have to go back to Terenure for the rest of this school year,' I say.

'You can make it,' says Abigail. 'Now you know there is hope.'

Fingers crossed she is right.

CHAPTER 16

An Emergency Exit

1989 (age nine)

Abigail is right, there is hope, and I cling on to it, but sometimes it's just not enough to keep me going. Today is the day things really come to a head. Today is the day I finally exit this world. I know I told Mam I would talk to her before I made any decision to leave, but it all happened so fast, there wasn't time.

I'm lying in bed listening to my alarm clock beeping, its plastic frame vibrating, demanding that I press the little button back down.

Unlike most digital alarm clocks, mine only has one button sticking out of the top. You press it to set the alarm and it pops up when the time comes. So, it isn't the alarm sound as such that wakes you but that of the plastic button shooting up, which, when you're asleep, sounds a lot like a door slamming shut.

I am very familiar with banging doors as I live in a house where doors are regularly slammed with anger, and sometimes if it's late at night and I'm asleep, I am often confused as to why my alarm has woken me at that moment.

Because I share the downstairs bedroom with Simon, and because I am younger than him, I sleep on the bottom bunk of the red bunk bed John built out of left-over timber he acquired from a site or job he was working on. The morning routine is that the alarm wakes me, then I turn on the lights to wake Simon. If any part of the sequence fails, the knock-on effect results in both of us being in trouble, so I take my role as alarm-setter very seriously.

But on this particular January morning, my brother isn't in his bunk bed. Being free from the social and emotional problems that plague me, Simon's friends aren't invisible, and so from time to time he stays over at theirs. Something that I can only imagine, and never experience.

I open my eyes and switch off the alarm. If I had known that this was the last morning I would wake up in the driving seat of my body, I may have taken a moment to appreciate the sounds of the outside world seeping in from our window.

I slide out of bed, step onto the carpet and enjoy feeling it between my toes, and wonder what the day will be like. For some reason my parents put cream-coloured carpet throughout the house, including our bedroom. I think John had come across a deal somewhere and, being the thrifty man he is, decided to put it down everywhere.

I leave the bedroom and tread warily along the hallway to the kitchen, listening out for raised voices and giveaway noises. To get from my bedroom to the kitchen, I need to walk past the stairs, but the problem is that the stairs lead directly up to my parents' bedroom. If, when passing by, you are suddenly caught in the crossfire of a huge shouting match between them, you don't have a lot of time to get out of sight. Therefore, once you have committed to passing the stairs you have entered the area of no return until you make it safely to the kitchen. My anxiety always peaks walking past the stairs.

I keep my eyes fixed upwards to check if they're about to come down. There is no sign of them, and I start breathing more easily when I get to the kitchen. But the door is shut. It's not usually shut. I stand there, my hand on the handle, deciding if I should risk opening the door.

From the other side I hear a cup hit the wall with a loud crash, followed by shouting, and then a second crash when the cup bounces off the wall and smashes on the ground.

The shouting gets louder, and I make the quick decision to retreat to my room.

Hiding under my bed in the shadows, I hear the kitchen door open. The footsteps on the creaky floorboards send signals to me like Morse code. Suddenly I am a dispatcher in a war room, deciphering the incoming messages and trying to gather as much information as I can in order to prepare for a possible incoming situation. I look over and see Giselle, my co-dispatcher in our bunker. Her headset is so big that it's wrapped over her forehead, almost blocking her face. She is, after all, only nine years old and military equipment isn't really child-sized. She gives me a reassuring look.

The floorboard creaks are so loud now that we don't need to strain to hear where the Enemy is coming from. I start to pull myself out from under the bed thinking it's better to be found in the open than to be discovered hiding. But Giselle gestures for me to follow her deeper into the darkness, deeper into the shadows under the bed and into Domdie.

I'm about to follow her into the darkness, but then I see the handle to my bedroom door begin to turn. I hesitate, not because I am afraid, but because I sense that if I follow her, I may never want to come back this time. There isn't much time to act.

I am now standing on the threshold of both our worlds.

Even though I have let Giselle take control of my body before and for increasingly longer periods lately, and although I feel more at home in Domdie than I do in this world, I am scared of completely giving over. At the same time, I realise that if I follow Giselle, I can live free from the enemies of this world. I wouldn't ever have to wake up to the sound of a broken alarm clock reminding me of my broken life, which is how things have felt.

I take a deep breath and prepare to submerge myself completely when I feel another hand on me. It is a bigger, colder hand than Giselle's. A hand with no connection to me. The Enemy has found me hiding, and I am being pulled out of my bunker. Giselle reaches out to me again, but it is too late.

I allow my body to go limp and show no resistance, to ensure a better outcome. Giselle is still under the bed, wearing her headphones and watching me being dragged out. We have been in this situation many times before; she retreats to the safety of her world, and I embrace the punishment of mine, and then we regroup later. But this time she isn't withdrawing, she is reaching out her hand to me again. I take hold of it as she emerges from the under the bed.

John is shouting at me now. He is twice my size and casts a large shadow over me. He leans in closely as he always does so I can feel him, feel his rage, his breath and his spit as it lands on my face. He is gripping my arm so tightly that our union is physical and real and yet at the same time, I can't hear him anymore, I only hear a slightly muffled echo of the words I have heard a hundred times before. The louder he shouts, the stronger Giselle squeezes my hand.

He raises his arm and strikes me; I feel her energy transferring from her hand to mine. He strikes me again, the hairs on my neck are beginning to stand up, our hands gripped tighter, my eyes fixed ahead.

He strikes me again.

This time the force is so hard that my tiny nine-year-old body has no chance of withstanding his power. I stumble backwards. I always try to remain steadfast when enduring the Enemy's wrath as weakness might encourage him to be even more violent. Still holding onto me, Giselle reaches down into the stream and, using her free palm to scoop some fresh water, she offers me a drink. Am I thirsty?

He strikes me again.

I can feel my body losing its balance. The only way I can stop myself from falling to the floor is to let Giselle's hand go and catch myself on the bed, but I'm more afraid of losing our connection, so I let myself fall.

I'm lying on the floor on the cream carpet beside my bed. He is standing over me, still shouting, but something is different. There is a flow of energy travelling through me now. What started out as a tingle in the palm of my hand is growing bigger and bigger as Giselle and I are holding on to each other. It's in my feet now, it's rushing to my head . . . I've forgotten where I am.

I look up at the sun as it's setting in Domdie; its rays are glimmering over the mountains in the distance, it's trying to make the most of these last moments of this day, spreading its warmth and light as it slowly descends. I can smell the fresh cut grass and I can hear the birds. The sound of the river flowing brings a sense of peace.

I can't see the Enemy anymore, I don't know where he is. I know that the time has come – that the power of Domdie is allowing me to hand over full control of our body to Giselle, and not just for a few minutes like we have done so many times before. This feels different, like it might be permanent, and I'm fine with that.

Now, I'm just an observer in the real world. I can feel Giselle standing back up, a lot more confident than I could have been in this moment on my own. Ready for impact, she is going to take my pain so I can be protected, but he doesn't strike. I'm not sure why, maybe he senses a change in me, maybe he doesn't want to hit a girl. He never hits either of my sisters. He turns and walks out of the door. Giselle walks over to the fireplace and looks into the mirror above it. We can see each other; it is amazing to be on the other side.

I think I will stay in Domdie, where it's safe.

The following day, I wake up and hear a beautiful tune being played. I am sitting by the river, watching my reflection. It's warm in Domdie today – not sunny, not cloudy, just warm. There is a summer breeze blowing across my face. I dip my toes into the water, creating ripples.

I feel bad that Giselle isn't here with me to enjoy this moment of peace. I don't know how to resolve this so that she isn't trapped there, instead of me.

'How can I be free?' I ask Abigail. 'How can I be me, without trying to hide?'

She looks over with her sisterly loving eyes, and says, 'You can be free, but you must choose your adventure. Life can be full of pain, but pain is what reminds us that we're alive.'

I wonder if you can feel pain if you're in some kind of emptiness, in some kind of void.

'Where would you go if I'm not here?' I ask out loud.

'I don't know,' she replies. 'I was invisible, until you made me visible.' She looks down at her hands. 'So, if you go away, I guess I will be invisible again.'

I am thankful that Giselle is driving the skin machine

right now and allowing me a break from my life so I can get used to the idea of leaving for a bit longer before I make this irrevocable decision.

I wonder what I will miss the most.

I know I will miss my brother, and the bond we share as allied battlefield soldiers, fighting the same Enemy. He has found a way to express himself, a way to cope, but I have not. I will miss the smell of the world, the simple taste of water and the feeling of excitement on Christmas Eve, lying in bed wondering what tomorrow will bring.

I feel paralysed and incapable of making a decision. I have to allow Giselle to carry on taking over. Then I shall know if I am ready to go back.

CHAPTER 17

A Betrayal

1989 (age nine)

It's a cold evening, and I am hiding under the old yellow boat resting at the top of our driveway. I am wet from the rain-soaked grass underneath, but I must remain quiet and vigilant if I am to escape. I am hiding from the Enemy, under his own boat. He bought it a few months ago with the intention of taking Jonathan fishing, but that never happened, and it has remained here in this very spot since it arrived.

Jonathan is safe in Domdie. He is so disconnected from the real world that he's stayed there, and I – Giselle – am doing what I need to do as him to use my time here to help him. I know he wouldn't have the courage to run himself. But I am in control now, and I am not afraid of the Enemy.

'Have you found him yet?' I hear a voice shout.

'Who's that?' I ask Abigail.

'It's Grampa, Giselle,' she replies.

'Not yet,' John replies, 'but I'll fucking kill him when I find him. This is typical Jonathan.'

Clearly, John has called his parents to see if that's where I have gone, knowing that's where Jonathan ends up when he's hiding from trouble. But this time I was worried they would return me to him. So instead, I hid here, to give me some time, to think of a plan.

We listen out to hear if the voices have moved on, but the wind obliterates all sound, so I am finding it hard to track their movements.

'Is it safe to move?' I ask Abigail.

I lean down to peak out from under the boat. As I slowly start crawling out on my stomach, placing the weight of my body on my arms, my jumper gets completely soaked.

Directly in my line of vision is John's shoe. They hadn't moved away, they'd just stopped talking. I freeze, I don't want them to see me.

'Where else would he go?' asks Grampa.

'He is probably off on one of his daydreaming walks,' replies John, seething.

'They didn't see us,' whispers Abigail, as I crawl back under the cover of the boat.

'How's Brid taking this?' asks Grampa.

'She's at the pool as usual, so she doesn't know.'

'Do you think he could have gone to her?' continues Grampa.

'No, I bet he is just wandering around somewhere,' John answers. 'He is so bloody sensitive all the time, I don't know what to do with him. He gets upset about everything.'

He pauses.

'I've tried to reason with him, I've tried to talk to him, Dad. But it's like I can't get through. It's like, sometimes, he isn't even in there.'

Grampa's tone is warm, calm and reassuring, 'He's just a little fella, he probably just doesn't know how to talk to you about what upsets him. I'm sure he will come back soon.'

I hear them walk back into the house and spot my moment to flee. I crawl back out from under the boat and hide in the shadows, covered in mud and grass. I look quickly back towards the house to make sure I've not been spotted. I linger on my bedroom window, the curtains still drawn. This might be the last time I see this house. I run.

I don't know where I am going, or where might be safe. And then I remember a speech a priest gave once when we went to mass with John, back before the Enemy had fully taken him over. When we would stand at the back of the church, and he would rub Jonathan's head affectionately.

'He was so much fun back then,' I say to Abigail as we half-walk, half-run down the road. 'I wonder what changed him. I wonder what life would have been like for us, if he'd stayed the same.'

'Would we even be here,' wonders Abigail, 'if Jonathan didn't need us?'

'I remember the happier times,' I say, 'so I think we were always going to be here, but maybe not as saviours, more like friends.'

I decide that going to see a priest is a good idea. He talked about God being salvation, and he is God's friend, so he must be salvation too, I conclude. And I really need to save Jonathan.

I know there is a priest in the next street, because I have often seen him outside, cutting his hedge, dressed in his black shirt and trousers. On Halloween, Simon's friends, who usually cause trouble by throwing fireworks at people's doors, always avoid his house out of fear of being struck down by God. Surely once I tell the priest of Jonathan's struggle, he and his God will save us.

The priest's front door is a carbon copy of mine.

'Isn't it strange how this door looks the same as our door, but behind it is a whole different world?'

'We don't know what's on the inside yet,' cautions Abigail.

I can't reach the doorbell, as I am small, even for a nine-year-old. There is a brass knocker, which I use instead. The sound echoes into the night and I worry that this noise is going to attract the wrong kind of attention.

After a moment, I hear a voice from inside.

'Hello?' It's the priest. The porch light comes on and the door opens slowly. The priest is dressed but he's rubbing his eyes like he's not quite awake yet.

'We need help,' I say, shivering in my wet clothes.

The priest looks beyond and around me.

'Who's "we"?' he asks, confounded by the soggy mess in front of him.

'I mean me, I need help,' I reply.

'Well, come in out of the rain, son, you're soaked!' He opens the door further and invites me in.

I step inside his hallway. It is lovely and warm. On the wall there are pictures of Jesus and other religious paintings. There is the smell of freshly brewed tea and candles in the air. He directs me to his sitting room and offers to make me a cup of tea as I take a seat on his sofa. He disappears into the kitchen.

I look around. The sitting-room is like the hallway with lots of art on the walls, which are covered in red floral wallpaper. There is a small grey television and a cabinet next to it that showcases several small religious statues and a white cup with the Dublin logo on it. It is from last year's millennium celebrations when Dublin turned one thousand years old.

I remember that warm July evening; John had woken the kids a few hours after they'd gone to bed and put all four of them into the back of his car to drive them into the city centre. I had never seen the city at night, nor had I ever seen such a display of patriotism. People lined the streets with flags of Dublin and shouted and sang in unity over the special event.

At school, the millennium had been all anyone talked about, the art and history classes had this as its singular focus. And a few days after that, Dublin gave someone named Nelson Mandela a key to the city.

'Do you think it's a good idea to have a key that opens everyone's door?' Jonathan had asked.

'He lives very far away so he probably won't use it,' I said, having heard about Nelson on the television, and how he was also trapped in a place he didn't want to be, and wasn't allowed say how he really felt without being punished.

When the priest comes back, he has a mug of tea and a small plate of biscuits for me. He sits down in the armchair across from me.

'So, tell me what's wrong,' says the priest as he leans back into his chair. He has a peace about him that makes me feel trusting and willing to share. 'But first, what's your name, son?'

'Jonathan,' I reply, on his behalf.

'And your surname?'

'Joly. My house is near here' I say, 'but I don't want to live there anymore.'

I take one of the jam-centred biscuits he has laid out for me. We don't have fancy biscuits like this at our house, so things are already looking up.

'Sometimes,' he says as he takes a sip of tea, 'things seem worse in our heads than they actually are.'

He pauses, to gauge my reaction, but I don't let on if I agree with him or not.

'I'm sure it's not that bad,' he continues, and I notice that he is trying to look at his watch discreetly. 'It's probably some sort of mix-up,' he says as he leans forward. 'Have another biscuit,' he says gently, as he picks up the plate and holds it out for me.

I don't take another one. I'm suddenly feeling sad and very lonely. How can I make people understand what Jonathan is going through?

'It's not in my head,' I say.

The priest continues to hold out the plate, saying nothing but expecting me to give in and take one. I want one too but if I take one and start eating it, I will look happy, and then he will think I don't need the salvation that he talked about.

'He hits me,' I say, looking directly into his eyes without breaking my stare. 'And shouts at me and calls me names.'

I'm aware I'm speaking a little louder now, because I am worried he isn't taking me seriously. 'I don't want to go home, I'm too scared.'

He must be hearing the panic in my voice, because he puts down the plate, and says: 'It's okay, you can stay here as long as you like, Jonathan.'

He gets up and tells me he is going to get some more tea, even though I haven't drunk any of mine yet. I wait until he has left the room before talking to Abigail, as I am worried that because of his godly ways he might hear our conversation, and then maybe he won't help us.

'As long as we like, he said,' I say to Abigail. 'We can stay here in this house and eat biscuits!'

'You can't live on biscuits,' says Abigail, looking at the plate on the coffee table.

'I wonder which bedroom will be ours? I think Jonathan will be happy here.'

Abigail can't help getting excited about the idea.

'It is pretty close to his old house, so he will be able to see Simon, Ruth and Leah all the time too,' she says.

'Maybe they can come and live here with us,' I say, and I finally give in and take another biscuit.

As I start munching, I hear the musical tune of a doorbell. There is someone at the door, and it's clearly not a small child like me who can only reach the brass knocker.

The penny hasn't dropped yet, and I still believe we are safe until I hear John's voice. I freeze. I can't swallow my mouthful of biscuit. The priest comes back in.

'He's in here,' he says, as he leads John into the sitting room.

'Thank God,' utters John as he comes over to me and wraps his arms around me. 'We were all worried sick about you.'

He is speaking in a hushed tone. 'Don't ever do that again, Jonathan,' he adds.

'I'm glad it all worked out,' says the priest, still standing in the sitting room doorway. 'You can take the biscuits home with you, son.' He smiles at me.

I stand up, still wet, and after grabbing a few more biscuits, follow John out of the sitting room. Maybe the biscuits are the salvation so we can taste the sweetness of life for a brief moment, before things turn sour again. The priest accompanies us down the hallway to the front door.

'You're welcome anytime, son,' he says, as he waves us goodbye. There is nothing in his face that shows regret or fear for Jonathan. He thinks he has done the right thing: reunited a father and a son. And why would he be worried? John is clearly distraught, and relieved to see his child. But I know an attack is coming. There is no way the Enemy will allow this to stand, allow me to talk about what goes on behind closed doors to someone outside the family.

As we step through the squeaky gate and into the road, I brace myself. But then an unexpected thing happens: instead of shouting, John speaks softly to me.

'Why are you so upset all the time, Jonathan?' he asks.

'I don't know,' I reply, fearful of giving him any information.

'You know you can always talk to me, if you're down,' he says. 'I love you.'

This is very confusing. Usually after something like this, he goes crazy before calming down again. It makes me wonder whether John really can change, and if he can, maybe there is hope that one day Jonathan can return. I know things will get better at school once we start at St Declan's and maybe if life at home becomes less stressful too, with fewer encounters with our Enemy, then maybe this world will become suitable for Jonathan to come back to again.

CHAPTER 18

Coming Home

1990 (age ten)

Things are different now.

Jonathan is still safe and sheltering in Domdie and I have done my best to make life better for him in the real world over the last few months. The days don't seem as dark anymore, and not just because it's almost the summer. The small changes I have made for us have brought some much-needed light into our life even though our Enemy still appears from time to time. When things get hard in school, I just leave our skin machine on auto pilot and join Jonathan. We don't have long left at Terenure, so we are riding it out, playing in the never-ending fields and valleys in Domdie. We love to sit by the river and talk about our feelings, and today we have a surprise for him.

'I don't believe you,' says Jonathan, dipping his toes in the cool water as he always does.

'It's true, I promise,' I reply.

'We thought you needed a friend in the real world,' says Abigail. 'Someone you can feel connected to if you ever return.'

'What's their name?' asks Jonathan, beginning to sound excited.

'Benji,' I say, 'he's a boy.'

'Like the dog from the television show?' Jonathan teases with a smile.

'Yes, because I want a talking dog, like the alien prince Yubi has,' I joke. 'I would also like a droid like Zax, but I don't think that's possible.'

'But a talking dog is totally possible,' adds Abigail, laughing.

'But how?' asks Jonathan.

I had been on one of my walks, on auto pilot while I was playing with Jonathan in the woods, and after I had taken back control, I was not entirely sure where I was. I had taken a turn off Greenly Road and come out the other side on Kimmage Road. I hadn't done that before, so I felt kind of lost.

While I was standing at the side of the road looking up and down, trying to decide which way to go, I heard a whimper from inside a bush near me. And when I pushed the branches and leaves aside, I saw a little white dog sitting in there. She looked sad and was making strange sounds.

I picked her up and carried her back to our house. I got lucky that Mam and John were both at work, so I was able to sneak her into my room. I managed to get away with having her for over a day, by feeding her half my dinner, until she was eventually caught barking in the night.

'And they let you keep her? Wait, didn't you say the dog was a boy?' says Jonathan, looking puzzled.

'No, I wasn't allowed to keep her,' I reply.

The day her owner came to collect her I was very upset about letting her go and couldn't stop crying. The owner told me the dog was about to have puppies, and, as a reward for saving her she offered to let me choose one. To my surprise, John and Mam said yes. So now we really do have an actual puppy called Benji!

'You'll love him,' I say to Jonathan. 'He is very funny, but also totally misunderstood, just like us.'

Benji tries to bite anyone who comes near him, especially when he is eating. But for some reason, he never bites me. He spends half his day chasing his own tail, running in circles and barking at shadows. But he is my friend, and to me there are no negative sides to his personality. He listens to me, sits with me when I am sad, never calls me names or makes me feel different. Mam and John fight a lot about what to do with Benji, just like they fight about what to do with me.

Then another change happens. It is the day of a major football match, and John and Mam have invited friends over to watch. They want to open up the partition between the dining room and the playroom, so that everyone can fit. I am tasked with tidying up the playroom. Even though I don't like interacting with other people, I don't mind when guests come over because we all act like a loving happy family. A break from the heavy atmosphere at home is always welcome.

'This is going to take for ever,' I moan, looking around at the displaced board games and scattered playing cards. The Monopoly money is mixed in with the Game of Life money and all the Guess Who picture cards are jumbled up with the Cluedo name cards.

'How are you going to separate these out?' giggles Clarence, looking at the pile of Campaign game pieces, strewn among the coloured plastic Bed Bugs. 'Who even plays Campaign anyway?' she continues, chuckling to herself, looking at the red box with a picture of a sword, some armour, and a military hat. '8+, it says here. I don't think anyone under the age of fifty would play this.'

Clarence is the newest addition to our friendship circle; she is fun and full of life. It used to be me making the jokes, I was the comic relief in our invisible group, but I've got a new job now – trying to make things safe for Jonathan so that he can come back – so I can't fill that role any more. And then a few weeks ago, Clarence just showed up one day as we were playing in the wooden fort at Marley Park.

'Why not just stuff all the boxes and bits into that cupboard over there,' she suggests, pointing to the large brown cabinet in the corner.

'It's not a bad idea,' I acknowledge. 'It would save us a lot of time.'

'Are you sure?' says sensible Abigail. 'What if someone opens the cupboard to get something?'

'Who's going to go looking in there?' replies Clarence, standing by the cabinet, amused by the idea of someone ever needing anything from inside it.

I really don't want to spend my entire day cleaning this room, so I figure I will listen to Clarence, and quickly just stuff everything into the drawers and cupboards and hope nobody opens it. I have just about completed my job when John enters, carrying the new television that he is planning to place on top of the cabinet so that they will be able to watch the match while sitting at the table.

'Good stuff,' remarks John as he walks into the now-tidy room. 'I knew you could do it if you put your mind to it.'

John has been saying many more positive things to me lately. During one of my preparatory meetings for my transfer from Terenure to St Declan's, I overheard Father Andrews instruct John and Mam to treat Jonathan better and understand that he sees the world differently and that his mind works differently, so they need to have more patience with him.

Father Andrews also gave them a list of foods Jonathan was no longer to have: basically, anything with an E number, artificial colouring or sugar was off the menu for him. Watching television was also on the 'bad' list, as apparently that could affect his attention. Jonathan will be very sad about that, because he loves watching other people's lives and being introduced to different worlds. I know that reading a book is hard for him: the words on the page still jump around, so he finds it hard to follow the story and gets frustrated with himself. This doesn't happen when he watches television.

Mam and John applied this advice to Ruth, Simon and Leah too, who are also not happy with these changes. I don't think they know it's because of Jonathan; whenever I've heard them complain about how we never have anything nice to eat in the house they don't seem to blame him.

'Give me a hand with this,' John says, as he places the television down on a table. He doesn't usually ask me for help with technical tasks since I'm not so good with them, so I am pleased that he invited me to help.

'Grab this cable and stick it in the wall,' he says.

'Sure,' I say, taking the black cable from him. 'Do I just push it in here?' I point to the cable socket.

'Yes, perfect,' he replies.

The television comes to life as soon as I plug the cable into the wall. I stand back to admire my work. On the screen, there is a group of men sitting around a table, talking about the football match Mam, John and their friends are very excited about.

'Look what I did with John!' I say to Clarence and Abigail. 'Maybe it's time for Jonathan to come back.'

'Do you know where the remote is?' asks John.

'No idea,' I reply, looking around the clean room, admiring once again the fine job I've done.

And then he opens the cupboard to check if it's in there. As he pulls the handle back, the entire contents of the gaming room come crashing down onto the floor, exposing what I've done.

It all happens so fast that by the time I have a chance to turn and look up at him, John has disappeared and the Enemy is standing with closed fists, looking down at me with fury.

225

'For fuck's sake!' he screams. 'Can you not do anything right?' I can see his rage grow.

'It was an accident,' I plead, leaning down to start the clearing up again.

'You're the fucking accident!' he shouts at me. 'Come here!' He grabs me by the neck and wraps his arm around me, holding me in place. 'You fuck everything up,' he spits. 'I can't have just one fucking day without your messing.'

He lets me go and I fall to the floor, landing on all the puzzle pieces. I don't feel the small plastic objects as they poke into my skin. My body goes numb like it always does when I drift into auto pilot and join Jonathan in Domdie.

Jonathan is there, surprised to see me distressed. It doesn't happen so much lately.

'What's wrong?' he asks. I can barely speak. 'Giselle, tell me,' he insists.

Being here calms me down and I find my voice again.

'How will the world ever be ready for you if it never stops hurting you?' I say, worried that the cycle will never stop and Jonathan will never be able to return and I will have failed in my promise to make the world better for him.

'Just forget that world,' says Clarence, as she joins Jonathan on the swing next to him.

Abigail joins us by the swings, as all four of us think about not going back.

'No,' I say. 'That's not the answer. I'm going to go back and fight for us,' as I get back in control of the skin machine. I open my eyes. I am still lying on the floor with the Enemy standing over me, shouting.

I find an inner strength that suddenly propels me up and I stand up to confront him. Something in me has snapped.

'Enough!' I shout.

There is a pause.

'What's enough?' he shouts back at me, stepping closer. 'I'll fucking show you enough!' And he raises his fist.

I call out to my friends in Domdie.

'Help me!'

It is the moment that turns the tide. With our combined strength, we push the Enemy back with one big push to the floor, letting out a roar as we do so.

'Enough!' we all shout, standing over him.

Suddenly the Enemy that has terrified us for years doesn't look as scary as he lies on the floor. He looks stunned that a ten-year-old boy has managed to knock over a forty-year-old man. I don't wait to find out what happens next, I just walk out of the room and retreat in victory to my bedroom.

'I can't believe you did that!' says Jonathan, admiring the power I have just wielded.

'*We* did that,' I correct him, '*we* defeated our enemy,' as all four of us stand together, smiling at each other. 'You were there too, you know.'

I look at Jonathan.

'Maybe it's time you come home,' I suggest. 'Maybe this time things really will change.'

There is a moment of reflection as we all watch the sun set on another day in Domdie, its orange hue fading into the background. It's a glorious moment of quiet after the storm. It might be too early to say for sure, but it does feel like something really might have shifted.

'Okay, I'll give it a try,' he says to me.

CHAPTER 19

Time to Let Go

1991 (age eleven)

'Hand me that spanner,' says Dave, as we stand under the car.

I've been working as a sort of apprentice at Dave Curry Motors for a while now. It began as a summer job last year, right before I started in St Declan's, because the school suggested I do something useful. As my parents are friends with Dave, a local mechanic, he took me on. I overheard John saying to him that this is also a back-up plan because he doesn't think I will amount to much, even if I do manage to complete school. He thinks working here will teach me a trade, and then hopefully that will lead to a job someday. This is my second summer helping Dave.

In the last year, the Enemy has been less present. He still

appears from time to time, but I no longer need an emergency exit to deal with him. At St Declan's I have a meeting once a week with Father Andrews, during which he asks me lots of questions about my feelings. I know he is still talking to my parents too, which I think is what's improving the situation at home even more.

Dave and I are in the pit while he does an oil change on the Honda Civic above us. I am supposed to be learning from him, but I am too distracted by Giselle. 'This must be what's it is like to be run over by a car,' says Giselle, looking up at all the metal pipes running from the engine to the exhaust. I've learnt that the underside of a car is the unseen structure that makes it all happen, just like humans and their organs and bones on the inside. You can't see them, but you know they're there, doing all the work. If you do see them, it's never good news.

'Earth to Jonathan,' says Dave, getting annoyed that I haven't got him the tool he asked for.

'Sorry,' I say, as I hand him the spanner.

I know the reason for me being here is not about the money, but the five pounds a day I've been earning is about to be put to good use. I've had my eye on buying my very own hi-fi system so that I can play the music Giselle and I want to listen to. I never used to care much about music, but lately I find it's like a soundtrack to Domdie: a way for me to feel like I am there whenever I want, but still be *here*.

I have made several friends at school – some girls, but also some boys. They are more like me and less like the boys that used to pick on me. When I'm not hanging out with them, I'm playing with Benji in the garden.

Before I know it, summer is over and it's the start of term again. There's a new boy in our year. It's Seán, one of the bullies from Terenure, who has been transferred to St Declan's, following in my footsteps. The school saw the positive changes in me and is now sending all the lost children here.

It's the first day, and he is alone and nervous, standing in the playground at break time like a confused little sheep. It crosses my mind that I could pick on him and mock him as he used to with me. I remember the pain and humiliation I felt that day when he kicked me in the head as I was walking out of school. Falling to the ground didn't end my suffering, it only made it worse, as Mr Williams came over and mocked me further as he often did.

'This could be your opportunity to get revenge,' whispers Clarence. 'We've defeated the Enemy at home, and now we can defeat an old enemy from school.'

I walk over to Seán, flanked by my real-world friends, Paul, Stephen, Emma and Jane. I am the one with a crew now, I am the popular kid who has the power to decide who is in and who is out.

'Hi, Seán,' I say, as he looks up and realises who I am. He doesn't look like the boy who once taunted me. In this environment he looks smaller.

'Push him over,' says Clarence.

'Joly,' he says, surprised. 'So, this is the school you went to.'

Near the end of my time at Terenure, my then-teacher thought it was a good idea to announce to the class that I was leaving.

'They do their lessons on computers,' he read out from the information booklet that Patrick had taken out of my bag and passed around the class until the teacher spotted it and took it for himself.

'A school for emotionally challenged children,' he read on.

He lowered the pamphlet and looked at me.

'Are you emotionally challenged, Mr Joly?' he called out to me in a condescending tone.

'More like mentally challenged, Sir,' Seán had said as the class erupted in laughter.

When I remember this, I think back to my feelings of shame in that moment. But though it is tempting, I'm not sure about taking revenge.

'And now you're here, too,' I reply.

'How do you know him?' Paul asks me.

I look over at Paul, and then back to Seán, who is looking slightly nervous, clearly wondering if I am about to reveal that he was once a tormentor. Clarence urges me again to humiliate him in front of my friends. But I still don't.

'He was at my old school,' is all I say.

'No way!' said Stephen. 'Were you friends?' He looks back and forth from Seán to me. I can see Seán has begun to clench up; he knows there is a possibility that all the abuse he has done to me is about to be thrown back to him. He knows I have no reason not to, and every reason to cast him out, like he did to me.

'Kind of,' I reply enigmatically, looking directly at Seán and leaving that hanging in the air, as if I am still about to reveal something. I'm not going to betray our past though; I don't want to be that person.

I reach out my hand to Seán. 'Welcome.'

He stands up, visibly surprised and relieved. Suddenly more confident, he begins to greet everyone, but makes sure to avoid me, just in case I change my mind. We go and play on the monkey bars and fill Seán in on silly school gossip, and we talk about my girlfriend Jennie, who I started going with a few weeks ago. I never really noticed her before, until my friend Emma told me she fancied me, so why not, I thought. I haven't spoken to her since that day she asked me to go with her, so it's working out well.

Seán comes over to me later, just before his class is called in. Even though we are the same age and were in the same year at Terenure, we are in different classes here. St Declan's wasn't structured the way other schools were: you came and stayed there for as long as you needed to, regardless of age. It didn't rank you based on your academic achievements but on your mental and emotional wellbeing. I was much further along with my personal development than Seán, and therefore in the year above him.

Surprisingly, he says, 'I just wanted to say I'm sorry for all the shit things we did to you,' as he kicks a stone next to a plant pot, not wanting to look at me. 'I was just going along with everyone else. You reminded me of me, so I wanted to hurt you.'

His voice starts breaking with emotion.

'I had no one to talk to. I hope you forgive me someday.'

He then turns and walks away, heading back to the school's main door. I think he is in tears and doesn't want me to see how much guilt he has been carrying all this time.

'He needs a friend like you,' I say to Giselle, remembering how she saved me when I was lost and disconnected. When I needed a friend to hear me.

Seán is hurting, but I don't want him to remain in his darkness, like the one he pushed me into. I want to set him free, even though he was once my enemy.

'Or,' says Giselle, 'maybe he needs a friend like you.' And we watch him enter the building.

Closing the Box

1994 (age fourteen)

The television is blaring out, so loud in fact that every inch of the house is subjected to its volume. Ruth, Simon, Leah, Mam, and I are watching it together.

'*Irlande*,' announces the French judge, and we all gasp.

'Ireland,' says the Irish presenter, translating, even though we'd all understood.

'*Huit points*,' the French judge continues.

'Eight points for Ireland!' the Irish presenter dutifully translates, unable to hide his excitement.

We hear a roar from outside the window as everyone in our road, and every road in our city, and the whole country at this moment, emits a loud and resounding cheer.

'That gives Ireland a total of two hundred and twenty-six points, which makes Ireland the official winner of the 1994 Eurovision Song Contest!' the Irish presenter shouts.

We all clap and whoop.

'We are rock and roll kids!' says Giselle, referring to the title of the winning song, 'Rock 'n' Roll Kids'.

'Shh!' commands Ruth. 'They're going to play again.'

Paul Harrington and Charlie McGettigan take to the stage and are given flowers by the presenters before they play the winning song once more.

Silence falls upon the audience as they know how historic this moment is: not only has Ireland won again, as we did last year with Niamh Kavanagh's 'In Your Eyes', but this is the first time in history that a country has won two years in a row.

The piano begins its musical melody of Irish patriotism, as Paul leans into the microphone and looks down the camera lens, knowing the entire country is watching. He starts singing about 1962.

'Do you remember '62?' I ask Mam.

'I was twelve,' she answers, 'of course I remember.' Her eyes are glued to the television. This is a special moment for us all.

'Did you have friends back then that you don't see any more?' I carry on with my questioning.

'I didn't really have friends growing up,' she answers, still watching Paul sing.

'I guess we have more in common than we thought,' says Giselle in my ear.

'I did have this one friend though, Arabella,' she continues, finally looking down at me. 'But no, I don't see her anymore. I guess we just drifted apart, happens to a lot of childhood friendships.'

'That will never happen to us,' I say reassuringly to Giselle.

'Friends for ever,' she replies, and she stands up and begins to re-enact a performance that had us mesmerised during the interval – something called *Riverdance*.

I left St Declan's at the start of the summer, just after I completed my third sacrament of initiation into the Catholic church. Father Andrews thought I was ready to re-enter mainstream education. Instead of going to work for Dave at his garage, like I had the previous summers, we moved to what feels like the middle of nowhere, outside the small town of Belmullet in County Mayo. Mam was offered a job working at an adventure centre, a place called Elly Bay.

The owners, Ciaran, who was still working full time as a pilot for the Irish Air Corps, and his business partner, John, an engineer from Cork, had applied for a grant to make Elly Bay an Irish-speaking college, where young Irish children could spend their summers mastering water sports and learning to speak Irish.

Part of the conditions of the grant required that a native Irish speaker be based at the centre for the summer. My mam not only had the Irish, but she was also a swimming teacher and a lifeguard, so she was the perfect candidate. My father didn't join us that summer, which made the whole experience conflict-free.

Our accommodation is a little yellow house next to a run-down barn, which is used to house all the water sports equipment. About a mile up the road is a pub which has a pool table and a little shop.

I have a summer job selling sweets at the little tuck shop inside the centre. It's inside a converted garage at the edge of the main house. I enjoy working there because I get to meet all the children that attend the camp, and most of them are the same age as me. Although I am much more confident than I've ever been, I still find it hard to strike up friendships in this kind of situation.

'Why don't you just become someone else?' suggests Giselle, as we look over at the small group of teenage girls hanging out near the shop.

'I don't want to be a liar, you know that,' I say.

'It's not lying, if you really do become another person,' she points out.

I want to walk over and talk to them, but I am worried about my past, about the person I am. Will I be enough? Will they notice that I'm different and dislike me for it?

'Who *would* they like?' persists Giselle.

'A cool, popular boy,' I reply, still staring at them from behind my shop counter. 'Someone who is happy in who they are, who doesn't feel like they're living a double life. Someone who doesn't carry sadness about them.'

'Then become him,' she suggests. 'Become the best version of the person you think people will like more, the person who lives the life you want, and then go and live that life.'

So, I did. That summer I projected a version of myself that was confident, open and happy. I changed from being someone clearly conflicted that everyone knew to tiptoe around, because of my emotional and learning difficulties. I knew I was different, I knew I didn't fit in, no matter how much people tried to adjust things for me. Instead, I did the adjusting for myself.

I rewrote my history and changed my present, no one knew my truth. These kids didn't know I'd been to St Declan's or that I had invisible friends or that I felt like a girl on the inside and had been bullied terribly my whole life. I threw myself into the summer's activities, I became popular, I had friends. I was nothing like the echo of my past.

One night, near the end of my time at Elly Bay, I snuck out of the yellow house. I walked down to the water's edge and sat on the sand next to Giselle. I needed to talk to her about what was around the corner, and I knew I wouldn't be able to sleep until I cleared a few things in my head.

'What will happen when we go home next week?' I ask her, thinking about my return to Dublin, and my return to the old Jonathan. I am scared of starting at another new school.

'You don't have to change back,' she replies. 'A new school, a new you.'

'But it's a boys' school again,' I say, 'and we know what happened last time,' remembering my time at Terenure College.

St Declan's had selected Rosmini in Drumcondra as a suitable secondary school for me, because a lot of former pupils had gone there and had success in completing their education.

'But you're different now,' she replies, 'you can be anyone you want to be. Look at how you managed this summer!' She sounds proud of me.

'But what if someone finds out about my past and all of my secrets?' I ask.

'You can lock your old life away in a box, and keep it closed, 'til you're ready to be you again.'

I wonder why I would ever want to open that box again.

The life I am living now is so far from that sad existence I once knew.

'Maybe someday the world will no longer need you to be adjusted, and you will no longer need to be someone else. You can become true Jonathan again,' she continues.

'But where would I even put this box? It needs to be somewhere nobody will ever find it.' I know if it is ever found out it could destroy me and everything I have now built around me to cope with the world.

'You can hide it in Domdie,' says Giselle. 'No one but you will ever find it there. In the meantime, you can be whoever you like, try them all on for size until you find one that fits.'

'Like an outfit,' I say, 'a different one for every occasion.' In my imagination, I am wearing fancy clothes, discarding them and replacing them depending on who I am with.

'Yes, and with different accessories too, depending on the role you're playing,' chuckles Giselle, thinking about all the times we dressed up in secret.

We both laugh a little and hold hands as the world begins to wake up. Then we make our way back to the dorm so that no one will notice we snuck out. I will return to this conversation with Giselle again and again throughout my life.

We head back to Dublin the following week and I join the new school shortly after. I put the plan in place and become someone new by watching television shows and movies, analysing the successes and failures of the characters and deciding which traits I should include in my new self. I observe real people on buses and in school and attempt to replicate their mannerisms and behaviour if they look confident and content. Giselle and I come up with a name for this: we call it 'taxiing'. Each of these people is a taxi that we climb into, heading to a new destination, and upon arrival we exit the vehicle and then proceed to find a new taxi to take us to our next stop, depending on our needs.

I do my swimming teacher's exam while trying out a sporting personality. It's made Mam even more proud of me. But as I look around my bedroom at all the shiny swimming medals I've won, I still feel an emptiness inside. And I know it's time to move on and get back into a new taxi. A friend at school called Brian introduces me to a street dancing club called Dance the Nations, and the manager has invited me to join. My next projection begins, and again I think this is where I will be happy. I form a band with another friend, Tim, this projection, too, might make me happy.

And so it goes.

The only thing I can't fix of course is my parents' relationship. They have changed their behaviour towards me, apart from taking my Benji away. I don't know if it was a punishment for standing up to him, or a solution to an even bigger problem that stemmed from my parents' relationship, but either way, Benji lost that battle, as he was taken to a vet and put to sleep. I was devastated. I made a promise to Benji after my father told me he was gone that one day I would grow up and fill my house with little white dogs, just like him, and give them the life he deserved.

Even though John is generally less angry, Mam and he still don't get on. But in November 1995, the divorce law is back in the news. It's come up again for review and another referendum has been called. It's the 25th of November, and today people are voting.

'Do you think anything has changed in the last nine years?' asks Giselle, remembering the results from the last referendum. I remember that night too, and what a scared little boy I was at the time. I don't need to hide in the shadows any more.

'We are getting some early numbers in,' announces the presenter on the television. It is Pat Kenny again, the same man who announced the results last time. But the broadcast is in colour and there are lots of graphics on the screen.

'Let's hope there is a different outcome this time,' I say to Giselle, holding her hand.

'The No vote count is eight hundred and nine thousand, seven hundred and twenty-eight, out of a total valid number of one million, six hundred and thirty-three thousand, nine hundred and forty-two votes,' he says.

'I can't do maths that fast,' I say to Giselle, trying to understand if the No vote is more or less than half the bigger number.

'And the Yes count is eight hundred,' continues Pat Kenny.

Then he pauses. Why is he doing this at a time like this?

'Sorry, I am just waiting for the numbers to be double checked,' he continues.

This doesn't feel good. Then Pat Kenny starts speaking again.

'Okay, I have it all sorted now,' he says. 'So, it's eight hundred and eighteen thousand, eight hundred and forty-two . . .'

'Wait, is that—?' I start saying.

'And so, with a margin of fifty-point-two-eight per cent to forty-nine-point-seven-two per cent, it's a YES to the fifteenth amendment of the constitution of Ireland.'

Giselle and I jump up.

'It's over!' I yell to Giselle, 'No more unhappy law!' as we clap our hands. Things are going to be even better now.

The next morning, I am heading to Galway with Mam to help with her swimming class. She has been working for a girls' school in Dublin called Loretto in St Stephen's Green, and as a treat she is taking her class to Galway for the day. It is a normal Irish morning, with the odd shower of rain and burst of sunshine, but something feels different.

'Ms Barton and I will do most of the planning, you can just mix in with everyone and help out as and when I need you,' Mam says to me as we arrive at Loretto's.

'Sure,' I reply, looking out of the window and wondering why I have butterflies in my stomach.

I board the bus and sit in the middle row next to a young girl named Ciara. I am in my element, surrounded by girls my age. I'm not afraid to talk to them and I am able to understand their emotions like they are my own.

'Blur or Oasis?' Ciara asks me.

'Blur,' I reply.

'He said Blur,' she whispers back to a girl sitting behind us.

'What's going on,' I ask. 'What's with all the questions?'

Ciara leans in conspiratorially.

'My friend really likes you,' she replies. 'Can she come up and sit with you?'

'Sure,' I say. Ciara gets up and walks down the bus, and then another girl comes up and sits next to me.

'Hi, I'm Una,' she says.

'Hi,' I say back.

'What other music do you like?' she asks. She's a bit flustered and fidgety.

'I kind of like all music,' I reply, trying to be mysterious and cool, like a character I have seen in a movie.

'Me too,' she says nervously.

'I like Counting Crows, because of the way their music makes me feel, but I also like East 17,' I say.

'Me too,' she says again. 'I'm actually going to their concert next week,' she continues, clearly trying to impress me.

'Me too,' I say. 'Maybe we should go together?'

'Ok,' she replies, smiling, and then she writes her home phone number on my hand with a pen someone passes to her from behind.

As I sit in companionable silence with Una, I tune into a conversation that Abigail, Clarence and Giselle are having. It's a conversation of such importance it takes me a while to understand its huge significance.

'He doesn't need us anymore, does he?' Abigail is saying.

'No, I don't think he does,' agrees Giselle. 'He's found a way to survive. We can let him figure it out without us now.'

'Will you go to Domdie?' asks Clarence.

'Of course,' replies Giselle. 'I can wait there for him if he needs me again, and you can keep an eye on him in the meantime.'

She sounds sad to be leaving.

'It won't be forever,' says Clarence, trying to be reassuring. 'He can visit you.'

This time, Giselle shakes her head.

'No. I will make him forget about us and I will close the box so he can move on, and be happy.'

It is at that moment that I realise what's going on.

'Wait, Giselle, you don't have to go!' But I know as I am saying those words that she will do what she feels is right.

'It's what's right. You will be safe here now,' she whispers as she starts to fade away, watching me carry on with my life without her.

And just like that, all my invisible friends are gone. I can picture them sitting by our river. I imagine them watching the sun set over the vast mountains. I can see Giselle lying down in the grass and closing her eyes.

I hear her voice.

'Till we meet again.'

'Till we meet again,' I answer.

And then I feel Una's hand slip into mine. I turn away from Giselle.

Acknowledgements

The first person I want to acknowledge is YOU; thank you for taking the time to listen to my story and for allowing me to sit with you and connect. Maybe you follow me on a social platform or maybe you have no idea who I am, but thank you either way (unless of course you are standing in a bookshop and have just flicked to the back of the book to see what it says . . . If that is you, then I recommend you buy this book, read it and I'll see you back here in a few days).

To my wife and best friend, Anna, who saw right though me from the moment we met and never tried to change me. You were the first (visible) person I was truthful with, and you didn't reject me. Thank you.

To my children, Emilia, Eduardo, Alessia and Andrea. Thank you for showing me what a family is.

To Jenny Heller, for hearing me when no one else did, and believing in me and my invisible friends. I couldn't have written this without your support.

To Katy Follain and the entire team at Quercus, thank you for helping me share my story with the world. Sorry my spelling was so bad.

To my parents, I hope this book helps to explain me a bit better. I'm sorry for being so difficult as a child; I had a lot to figure out. It only took me forty years, but I got there in the end.

To Ruth, Simon and Leah – sorry for being the reason we had no nice food in the house growing up. I wasn't sure I was ever going to own up to that, but I figured this might be the best time.

And finally, to Giselle, Florence, Abigail, Clarence and all the other invisible friends that played a part in my life, thank you for finding me, saving me and showing how I can help others just like me.

Just like YOU.